R.S. THOMAS
UNCOLLECTED POEMS

EDITED BY
TONY BROWN &
JASON WALFORD DAVIES

BLOODAXE BOOKS

ISBN: 978 1 85224 896 3

First published 2013 by
Bloodaxe Books Ltd,
Highgreen,
Tarset,
Northumberland NE48 1RP.

www.bloodaxebooks.com
For further information about Bloodaxe titles
please visit our website or write to
the above address for a catalogue.

Supported by
**ARTS COUNCIL
ENGLAND**

Cover design: Neil Astley & Pamela Robertson-Pearce.

Printed in Great Britain by
Bell & Bain Limited, Glasgow, Scotland.

I
Nancy, Sara ac Alys
a
Meinir, Mari a Rhys

ACKNOWLEDGEMENTS

As will be evident, tracking down poems from often obscure and sometimes short-lived journals, then the checking and re-checking of texts and publication details, has been a long process. In this time-consuming hunt for poetic needles in literary haystacks we have received invaluable assistance from numerous fellow readers of R.S. Thomas. In particular we are indebted to the indispensable bibliography of R.S. Thomas's published poems up to 1979 which was compiled by Sandra Anstey as part of her doctoral dissertation at Swansea University; we are also grateful to her for sending us some subsequent uncollected poems. In addition we very gratefully acknowledge the help, in various forms, which we received from John Freeman, Huw Ceiriog Jones, Morag Law, Kevin Perryman, Anne Price-Owen, Andrew Rudd, Meic Stephens, Graham Thomas, M. Wynn Thomas, Jeff Towns, Damian Walford Davies, Daniel Westover and Michael Whitworth.

CONTENTS

INTRODUCTION

No sooner had we started on the long process that has culminated in the present volume than, as ever, we discovered that R.S. Thomas was ahead of us with a cautionary note: 'Poems we threw up / too far back are not / to return to' ('Predicaments', 1981). However, when we began to study Thomas's uncollected poems – that is, those published in magazines, newspapers, journals, pamphlets etc., but not included in any of his collections – it immediately became apparent that there were in fact a significant number of poems from 'far back' that were indeed well worth 'returning to'. In fact, there existed a substantial body of work, from all stages of the poet's sixty-year career, that deserved to be reclaimed and brought to readers' attention. *Uncollected Poems* is a selection of what we consider to be the best of these 'lost' poems (a full list of the poems we have been able to identify is included in a bibliography at the end of the volume). While our main criterion in making a selection has been the quality of the poetry, we have also included poems which have particular autobiographical significance or which reveal aspects of Thomas's thematic and stylistic development. The poems are thus arranged in chronological order (and in alphabetical order within individual years). One of the effects of this arrangement, for instance, is to highlight the strikingly rapid evolution of Thomas's poetic style and the achievement of his distinctive voice in the years immediately following *Spindrift*, his first, unpublished, collection from the late 1930s. This arrangement, moreover, serves to emphasise the remarkable fertility of R.S. Thomas's poetic imagination in his final decades.

During the editing process we quickly became aware of recurring traits in Thomas's poetic practice – traits which occasionally presented the editors with interesting challenges when seeking to confirm that a particular poem had not in fact appeared in a collection. Unsurprisingly, there were those occasions when Thomas changed the title of a poem when including it in one of his volumes (for instance, 'Altars', first published in *Critical Quarterly* in 1971, becomes 'Echoes' when collected in *H'm* a year later). To complicate matters, a considerable period of time might elapse between a poem's initial publication and its inclusion, with a changed title, in a collection. For instance, 'Definitions', first published in *Poetry London* in 1982 becomes 'Opinions' in *Frieze* (1992), and 'The Idea', from *Poetry in English Now* in 1978, becomes *'Agnus Dei'*, part of the sequence 'Mass for Hard Times' in the volume of the same name in 1992. Another recurrent practice of the poet is the duplication of titles: for example, in 1978 Thomas writes two poems entitled 'Coming of Age', one of which is retitled 'Code' and published in *Later Poems* (1983), and the other retains its title and is collected in the present volume; there are also two different poems entitled 'Sonata in X', one published in 1973 and included here, and the other collected in *Mass for Hard Times* (1992). And in Thomas's autobiographical sequence, *The Echoes Return Slow* in 1988, the echoes do indeed return slow: several previously un-collected poems are here brought together by the poet, the earliest of which, 'Sick Visits' ('They keep me sober, / the old ladies'), dates back as far as 1962.

In reading this substantial body of rediscovered poems, several thematic concerns become apparent. Unsurprisingly, perhaps, one of the most prominent of these is the Matter of Wales. 'The Big Preachers' (1983), for example, sees Thomas revisiting Wales's Nonconformist past: on the one hand the poet gives us a sceptical portrait of these 'ranting captains pacing / their unstable bridges', while on the other he is aware that 'Those / were the imagination's heydays / and will not return'. In 'The Wisdom of Eliaser' (1969) – 'Done into Anglo-Welsh by R.S. Thomas', as the original pub-lication notes – we are in the grotesque world of Caradoc Evans ('Water proud now and much / water come soon long time / ... Duw but you make botch of it'). The period leading up to the Investiture of Charles Windsor as Prince of Wales in 1969 produces a series of responses, by turn angry, disappointed, bitter and dis-illusioned. Even Bardsey Island, reputedly the resting place of twenty thousand saints, becomes for the poet at this time 'a lavatory... / For the starlings that have their roost there' ('Ynys Enlli', 1969). Thomas's detailed knowledge of specific narratives of Welsh history is evident in a number of poems. 'Frontiers' (1964), for example, recalls Richard ap Howel of Mostyn's refusal to follow Henry Tudor to London after the Battle of Bosworth ('"I dwell with my own people"'); and 'The Return' (1967) makes symbolic use of the Welsh students at Oxford 'leaving their books / ... for the excitement / Of the border' and taking up arms as part of Owain Glyndŵr's revolt. Indeed, Wales itself takes on a number of guises in these poems. It is figured organically as 'the tree in the mind, / its foliage our language' in 'The Tree' (1983) – an image which invites us to recall that early poem of the same title from *An Acre of Land* (1952), a dramatic monologue in which, tellingly, 'Owain Glyn Dŵr Speaks'. Elsewhere, Wales appears (more problematically) in specifically gendered terms. In 'Feminine Gender' (1983), she is, variously, 'a face in chapel / ... raven-haired, / sallow of cheek', 'a bent / woman, too old to believe in, disfiguring / my sunlight' and 'a young girl, as innocent / as compelling', while in 'Cymru (Wales)' (1991), she is, uncompromisingly, a woman reduced to 'prostitution' and 'soliciting', recalling the poet Gwenallt's description of Wales as '[p]utain fudr y stryd' ('a dirty prostitute of the street').

We find a direct reference to Gwenallt (1899-1968) in the late poem 'Elders' (1996), where he appears alongside two of Thomas's Welsh literary heroes, Alwyn D. Rees (1911-74) and, crucially, that presiding presence, Saunders Lewis ('too small for his clothes, / too big for the strait-jacket / of our ideas'). Lewis (1893-1985), it seems likely, is the unnamed exemplar in 'Question' (1961), and is certainly the final figure of the roll-call of Welsh cultural heroes (Llywarch Hen, Owain Glyndŵr, Siôn Cent and Goronwy Owen) invoked in 'The Gallery' (again from 1996):

> he,
> the small man with the big
> heart, whom I met once
> in our pretending capital,
> taking my hand in both
> his and soothing my quarrel
> with my English muse with:
> 'But all art is born out of tension'.

Such poems are part of a surprisingly large group of 'pen-portraits', mainly of literary figures, and that 'tension' between Thomas's Welsh-language affiliations and his capacity to write poetry only in English is dramatised in a number of these character sketches. An important piece in this respect is 'Commission' (1955), in which the anguish of his own situation figures as a sub-text in his portrayal of the cultural choices made by his friend, the poet and critic Raymond Garlick: 'Welsh not by birth, but for a better reason – / Birth being compulsory and not chosen, / As you chose this: to live here and be kind / To our speech, learning it, and to our race'. This persistent creative tension between the language of R.S. Thomas's upbringing and education and his reclaimed Welsh-language identity is also strikingly evident in the presence of a gallery of English poets, from Tennyson ('Somersby Brook', 1954), to Betjeman ('Grass Platforms', 1981 – an evocative tribute to the man who provided an enthusiastic introduction to Thomas's first London collection, *Song at the Year's Turning* in 1955) and, later still, to Ted Hughes ('In Memory of Ted Hughes', 2007), a poet whose work had acted as a catalyst for Thomas's imagination, especially in the late 1960s. The unavoidable presence of the English tradition is wittily addressed in 'Poets' Meeting' (1983), where, in an *ymryson*, or poetic debate, several great poets – Wordsworth, Dunbar, Dafydd ap Gwilym, Aeschylus and Catullus – are seen engaged in a vigorous flyting session, only to be silenced at the very end by the appearance of Shakespeare, a 'figure / in honest kersey / poaching its dappled language / without protocol on the plain'. This acknowledgement of Thomas's profound imaginative debt to English poetry is directly voiced forty years earlier in 'Confessions of an Anglo-Welshman' (1943), where he admits that, while Wales's 'lore and language / I should have by heart', nevertheless

No patriotism dulls
The true and the beautiful
Bequeathed to me by Blake,
Shelley and Shakespeare and the ravished Keats.

14

The poem has hitherto not been collected: a confession, one might say, not fully confessed. Other personal confessions are vividly caught in a number of uncollected autobiographical poems. In 'The Father Dies' (*c.* 1978) – a piece never published during R.S. Thomas's lifetime – one senses deeply personal resonances, as the poet projects into the words of a dying father emotional inhibitions with which Thomas was himself all too familiar: 'I am not maudlin; / it is just that all my life / I tried to keep love from bursting / its banks'. But perhaps the most revealing poem here is 'Autobiography', published in 1973, the year in which the poet's mother died, and the year after he began to explore for the first time, in the autobiographical essay 'Y Llwybrau Gynt' ('Former Paths'), the familial and cultural elements that 'went to the making' of his own complex identity. Thomas looks back with a cold eye at what he sees as the bleak, limited lives of his parents before his own birth ('can't you see the emptiness / of their pockets / and their small hearts...?'), before turning to his guilty struggle to escape the inhibiting forces of his upbringing:

> I study to become the rat
> that will desert
> the foundering vessel
> of their pride; but home
> is a long time sinking. All
> my life I must swim
> out of the suction of its vortex.

More positive personal emotions are generated from the beginning by his relationship with Elsi Eldridge, to whom he was married for over fifty years. Among the earliest poems in the present collection are two that are addressed to her. In the sonnet 'I never thought...', which the poet included in his unpublished first collection, *Spindrift* (composed in the late 1930s), Elsi enters Thomas's poetic world for the first time: 'I never thought in this poor world to find / Another who had loved the things I love, /... One who

15

was beautiful and grave and kind, / Who struck no discord in my dreaming mind'. 'July 5 1940' was composed on the occasion of the poet's marriage to Elsi. Although the register and imagery of the poem betray the influence of the Georgian poets whom Thomas had been reading, there are nonetheless intimations here of the delicacy of tone – that 'soft weight' – that characterises many of his later love poems to Elsi. The poem ends with an expression of commitment, but tempered with a characteristic reserve: 'All of these, / A soft weight on your hands, / I would give now; / And lastly myself made clean / And white as the wave-washed sand, / If I knew how'. Thomas's later poems to his wife frequently set the firmness of the couple's love against the slow erosion of time and ageing. 'Birthday' (*c*. 1978), marking another stage in life's passing, is a moving example of this: 'Come to me a moment, stand, / Ageing yet lovely still, / At my side'. And in 'Luminary' (*c*. 1980), their 'gossamer / vows' have grown 'hard as flint, / lighter than platinum / on our ringless fingers'. The language in this remarkable poem is unusually extravagant for R.S. Thomas in its unambiguous celebration of his love for his wife:

> My luminary,
> my morning and evening
> star. My light at noon
> when there is no sun
> and the sky lowers. My balance
> of joy in a world
> that has gone off joy's
> standard.

As well as these poems of the private realm, Thomas continued to engage public and national issues in his poetry, though from the 1980s onwards with an added international dimension. He was, for example, consistently willing to contribute poems to publications in support of causes such as the Anti-Apartheid Movement, the homeless, Save the Earth and WaterAid. The drive towards technology, which Thomas had diagnosed four decades earlier in 'Cynddylan on a Tractor' in 1952 ('He's a new man now, part of the machine, / His nerves of metal and his blood oil'), had, towards the end of the century, become a global catastrophe. 'Oil' (1996) portrays humanity's ruthless urge – its willingness to engage in international conflict – to fuel capitalism's appetite for power. Here we see the Machine gone global, 'using those bones to divine / not water the soul / sickens without', but 'that other mineral, / smelling of corruption, of which / the whole world thinks itself in need'.

The act of bringing together Thomas's previously uncollected work reveals a series of patterns, correspondences, echoes and affiliations, not only between the poems within the present volume, but between these and the more familiar collected material. For instance, the uncollected 'The New Noah' was published in the same year, 1981, as 'The New Mariner' (from *Between Here and Now*), and the two can usefully be thought of as sister poems. The former expresses the loneliness of Noah in terms which directly echo – 'He blessed them' – that of Coleridge's Ancient Mariner, an allusion and identification more fully developed in the published poem. Several uncollected poems anticipate concepts, images and themes which are more fully developed in later works. A telling example would be 'Some Place' (1969), with its longing for what Thomas elsewhere terms 'the glimpsed good place' – 'Somewhere / There must be an area / Of calm, pure, clean / Air for the spirit / To inhale' – a site, indeed a state of mind, explored vividly as 'Abercuawg' in the following decade in both a poem and an essay. While another group of poems in this collection revisits the fields of Iago Prytherch, one poem in particular, 'Island Boatman' (1998), transposes R.S. Thomas's famous early protagonist into a new world, placing him in the seascapes of the poet's later years. The boatman, we would argue, is Iago Prytherch *redivivus*. Many of the poetic strategies employed in the Iago Prytherch poems are evident here, as the narrator views the figure from afar in the inclement weather, ponders the man's beliefs ('Was he religious?') and sits with him by 'a fire of salt wood, / spitting and purring' (compare the image of Prytherch's 'gobbing' in the fire in 'A Peasant'). And finally there is, as so often with Prytherch, ultimately a measured admiration:

I

forgave him his clichés,
his attempt to live up
to his eyes' knowingness.
They had looked down so many
times without flinching
into a glass coffin
at the shipwreck of such
bones as might have been his.

As R.S. Thomas completes his return journey to the seascapes of his youth, the poetry comes full circle.

TONY BROWN
JASON WALFORD DAVIES

UNCOLLECTED POEMS

The Bat

The day is done, the swallow moon
   Skims the pale waters of the sky,
And under the blossom of sunset cloud
   Is hidden from the eye.

And now when every spectral owl
   Is mindful of the ancient wars,
A withered leaf comes fluttering forth
   To hunt the insect stars.

1939

'I never thought'

I never thought in this poor world to find
Another who had loved the things I love,
The wind, the trees, the cloud-swept sky above;
One who was beautiful and grave and kind,
Who struck no discord in my dreaming mind,
Content to live with silence as a cloak
About her every thought, or, if she spoke,
Her gentle voice was music on the wind.
And then about the ending of a day
In early Spring, when the soft western breezes
Had chased the melancholy clouds afar,
As up a little hill I took my way,
I found you all alone upon your knees,
Your face uplifted to the evening star.

c. 1939

July 5 1940

Nought that I would give today
Would half compare
With the long-treasured riches that somewhere
In the deep heart are stored.
Cloud and the moon and mist and the whole
Hoard of frail, white-bubbling stars,
And the cool blessing,
Like moth or wind caressing,
Of the fair, fresh rain-dipped flowers;
And all the spells of the sea, and the new green
Of moss and fern and bracken
Before their youth is stricken;
The thoughts of the trees at eventide, the hush
In the dark corn at morning,
And the wish
In your own heart still but dawning –
All of these,
A soft weight on your hands,
I would give now;
And lastly myself made clean
And white as the wave-washed sand,
If I knew how.

1940

Confessions of an Anglo-Welshman

For my own country's part
Her lore and language
I should have by heart.
'Twas she who raised me,
Built me bone by bone
Out of the teeming earth, the dreaming stone.
Even at my christening it was she decreed
Uprooted I should bleed.
And yet for another's sake
No wound deletes,
No patriotism dulls
The true and the beautiful
Bequeathed to me by Blake,
Shelley and Shakespeare and the ravished Keats.

1943

Gideon Pugh

Gideon Pugh has a house of his own, but no wife
To ease the loneliness of his wide bed,
And the crickets, invisible under the cauldron
Of simmering broth, are a poor exchange for children
With their wearisome prattle on the bare hearth.
He works all day, his thoughts trained to one furrow,
A tattered pilgrim treading the indifferent earth,
But with darkness his mind is free, and the nights are long
Listening to the sound of the clock, sly as a mouse
Pattering to and fro in the still house.
The fire voice jars; there is no tune to the song
Of the thin wind at the door, and his nearest neighbours
Being three fields' breadth away, it more often seems
That bed is the shortest route to the friendlier morrow.

But for one whose feet shuffle their leisurely way
From hedge to hedge forty times in a day
With an indolent horse, there is surely a subtler reason
Than time or distance fastening him in his chair,
A dry bone of a man with moss-grown skull?
Could we lower the light, sharpen our eyes, peer
Beyond the mind's trellis, seeking the soul,
Small, shy as a flame of his own wood fire,
We would find – What would we find? For look! He has risen;
Our glib theories clutter our wits like burrs.
The door closes, he is out under the stars,
Braving the night's malice, the brown owl's mirth.

Follow him down, follow him down, he goes,
Drawn like a moth through the dark, to the far windows
To break the wings of his pride, sick with the hunger
No supper allays – But hark! Why does he linger
On the very fringe of the light? The problem returns,

And the night is in league, masking his haggard face
With its starved eyes brooding over the place.
Leave him, then, leave him alone with his secret dream,
The dream of a stone in the grass, the hunger of a tree
For the soft touch of the sky, of the land for the sea.

1944

Llanddewi Brefi

One day this summer I will go to Llanddewi,
And buy a cottage and stand at the door
In the long evenings, watching the moor
Where the sheep pasture and the shadows fall
Thick as swathes under the sun's blade.
And there I will see somewhere beyond the wall
Of the old church the moles lifting the ground,
And think of the saint's cunning and how he stood
Preaching to the people from his secret mound,
A head's breadth above them, and they silent around.

1948

Song

Up in the high field's silence, where
The air is rarer, who dare break
The seamless garment of the wind
That wraps the bareness of his mind?

The white sun spills about his feet
A pool of darkness, sweet and cool,
And mildly at its mournful brink
The creatures of the wild are drinking.

Tread softly, then, or slowly pass,
And leave him rooted in the grasses;
The Earth's unchanging voices teach
A wiser speech than gave you birth.

1948

Lines for Taliesin

I was at Catraeth, dazed with the grey mead
Like my lean countrymen. I saw them bleed
On the broad English plain, and heard their prayers
Falling unanswered on the indifferent air.

I was with Owain at Bryn Glas and knew
The frenzy of the victor. Swift winds blew
The storm clouds eastward, and my country lay
Chaste as a maid, asleep in the moon's ray.

The years have passed, and she lies dreaming still,
Where Caer Arianrhod gleams above the hill.
But dawn approaches, and Rhiannon's birds
Are busy in the woods. Hush! She has heard.

1949

Three Countries

At Soay of the Cuillins I saw the salmon leap,
Uneasy captives at the coble's side,
Where four stern men were hauling at the nets
That bore the glittering burden of the tide.

At Keem in Achill, when the nets were spread,
The basking sharks came cruising in the bay;
I saw the water broken by their fins,
And the bright eddies as they turned away.

But once in Malldraeth when the whitebait lay,
A serried harvest, in the grottoed shade
Of some green pool, I saw the mackerel fall
Softly upon them like a silver blade.

1949

Welsh Shepherd

Poor Iago Prytherch wandering in the dew,
Drunk with dew as others with wine;
Hanging out his thoughts on the far skyline,
Wind-chastened for the world to view.
At break of day behold him, alone with his few
Hedge-shorn yearlings and his bitch at heel,
A scarecrow of a man, becalmed in the unreal
Tides of light, with his cracked lips askew.

There he stands, counting his phantom flock
Carefully as his money, while the ravens mock
Each dream picture of a swollen fold.
A theme for sentiment? Yet spare your tears;
His speech is poetry, and the nimble airs
Of dawn have trimmed his tattered rags with gold.

1949

Y Gwladwr

Mae pawb yn gofyn bellach beth a ddaw
O'r byd sy'n troi ymaith o heulwen Duw
I edrych ar yr hirnos ddi-ben-draw,
Heb loer, heb sêr, a'u digyfnewid liw
Yn llethu'r meddwl. Ac mae pawb yn fud;
Nid oes gan hyd yn oed y doethion ddawn
Ond i roddi enw ar y dirgel hud
A rwyma'r enaid â'i angheuol wawn.

Ond ti, fy nghyfaill, efo'th lonydd braidd
Ar fryn a gwaun yn ymladd yn ddi-dor
Â'r ddaear ddidrugaredd, – caiff dy wraidd
Dy gadw di mwy rhag anorchfygol fôr
Y tywyllwch hwnnw, cans beth ond y tir
A all wneuthur dynion yn flynyddol ir?

1950

The Peasant

Everyone now asks what will become
Of a world that turns away from God's sunlight
To look at the endless night,
Without moon, without stars, their unchanging colour
Oppressing the mind. And everyone silent;
Even wise men have the ability
Only to label the dark mystery
That binds the soul with its deadly thread.
But you, my friend, with your peaceful flock
On hill and moor in constant battle
With the merciless earth, – your roots
Shall henceforth keep you safe from the invincible sea
Of that darkness, for what else but the land
Can make men eternally new?

[tr. Jason Walford Davies]

The Two Sisters

I know two sisters, dark and fair,
    So to compare them must be vain;
One is rich and shares the sunlight,
    And one the spleen of the grey rain.

The lands of one are sleek and green
    And wean men from their natural love;
The other tills a few lean acres
    Littered on the hills above.

She that is fair is soft of speech,
    Yet each smooth word conceals a lie;
From her I turn to where that other
    Keeps her cold vigil, proud but shy.

1950

Auguries

Do you know the light when the hedge leaves are thinned
By September gales? Prytherch knew it, too,
In the old days when he was a lad like you,
Following the plough cloudward, sowing the wind
With squalls of gulls at every furrow end.
Eyes greying with the dawn, boots bright with dew,
He walked these fields and gathered as they grew
The fresh mushrooms with the wet rind.
He saw also the armoured holly shine
Down to its spurs on many a matchless day
Of sunny calm, and took it for a sign
Of frost to follow with the bestial night
Coiled at its root. He read the sign aright,
But never dreamed how long the cold would stay.

1953

Darlington

Could the dead speak! Could the dead speak!
But they are quiet under the grass
That grows untarnished by their bones,
Quiet as their names upon the stones
That the moon traces with cold finger.

But stop a minute; under this mound's
Gathering tumour Darlington lies –
Those are snails that were his eyes –
A pale Saxon among the Welsh.
Lane wanderer, swiller of strong pints
In the mind's inn, knocker upon the door
Of countless imagined maidenheads,
He came a virgin to the grave's bed.

His life was lonely; his white cottage,
Small as a sheep upon the hill,
The bright hill under the black cloud,
Was bare as a box and brought nothing,
Not even a tree to tell the seasons by.

And now in death he has come down.
The hill at night no longer wears
Bravely his asterisk of light.
Yet the valley was deeper than he thought,
The grave less sociable; the Welsh dead
Keep to themselves; he is a stranger still.

1953

No Answer

Speak, farmer, over the green sod
To us forsaken by the sham gods
In whom we trusted. Where has the spring gone?
Is it always autumn even in the fields'
Primitive quiet in which you work?

Speak, friend; does not the earth renew
Its broken pattern, building again
Its green citadels, razed by the winds
And gaunt frosts, quarrying the face
Of the grim heavens for the spring's ore?
Born here and reared, have you no proof
Of the slow summer's ultimate reign?

Silence, silence; only the eyes'
Inscrutable greyness turned to mine;
And the hand's gesture, vague as a branch,
Rowing for ever the wind's stream.

1953

Peasant Girl Weeping

She cries, and her tears are the winter breaking
Not into spring, but into cold, colourless rain.
Her grief is a part of the earth's pain,
No less inscrutable, though less soon healed
Than the brief sadness of a bare field.
And after rain, when the sky clears,
And the wind chastens the wet airs
With a fine anger, the day is reborn,
And boughs that were sobbing forget the storm,
And the wood the way that its heart ached.
But she is a cloud whose gloom will lower
More darkly upon us after the last shower.

1953

Original Sin

It's no good talking of original sin
To the man in the fields with his half grin
Of natural shrewdness, whose blind fingers
Fondle the sex of the warm soil.

He thinks you're a fool; you think him wrong,
Despite the logic of a bird's song
From the bright hill, where the sun lingers
To bless softly his slow toil.

1954

Proportions

Walking in wide fields under a wide sky
He looks at nature, but not with your eye.
How differently? Different in kind,
Looking as a creature, where you look with mind?
Or different only in degree,
Seeing timber in the trees
Where you see beauty, the veined hand of God
Lifted to bless the despised sod?

1954

Somersby Brook

This brook was the pulse of his being;
I know; I have seen it,
An insignificant affair, stroking the grasses
In the drab fields.
But when the land is flat and there is nowhere to go,
No hill steep enough to sharpen the mind,
No wood darkening to an old legend,
One ignores the whole and prizes the parts,
Making a forest of the green cress,
A town of the trees' roots.

So it was then in his young life
Beginning at Somersby;
His thoughts were attuned to the brook's rhythm;
Its lithe movements, scaly with sunlight,
Startled his mind with a new joy.
And in the dark, if he leaned from his window,
It was as though the night spoke
In shrewd whispers –
And all because of this mean runnel,
Toying idly with a few stones,
Stones that became words in his verse,
Posed and polished in the mind's stream.

1954

A Welsh Ballad Singer

Thomas Edwards – Twm o'r Nant
If you prefer it – that's my name,
Truth's constant flame purging my heart
Of malice and of mean cant.
Out of the night and the night's cold
I come knocking at your door;
But not begging, my wares are verse
Too costly for you to set
Your purse against. Yet if you've bread
And cheese and beer and fresh cake,
I'll match them with as good a song
As you've an ear for. But take heed;
Muck of the roads is on my boots,
Dirt of the world clings to my tongue,
The mind's pool is quickly stirred
To bitterness. If you would keep
Bad thoughts from fouling the song's course,
Open your eyes' blue windows wide
And let me sample your smile's worth.

1954

Commission

(for Raymond Garlick)

Welsh not by birth, but for a better reason –
Birth being compulsory and not chosen,
As you chose this: to live here and be kind
To our speech, learning it, and to our race,
Who have God's pardon but have not His peace –
You know our grievance, know the bitter poison,
Black as despair, seeping from the wound
Your country dealt us; plead our rightful case
To those who come to us for what we give,
Who take and leave us ruined by their taking,
Since we must give in ways they understand.
They cannot see, the stale prerogative
Of history foists them on our luckless land;
Open their eyes, show them the heart that's breaking.

1955

Farm Wives

They were not beautiful, not fairies,
Though fairies called to you, the young
Women you took to be your wives
In high farms under the grey wall
Of cloud, where time is trapped in fields
Of stony grass that never changes
Spring and autumn its sharp tune.

I have seen them smirking, as I passed,
Toothless, busy with their brood
Of cats and chickens, heard their harsh
Voices calling in cow language
The heifers down from their thin diet
Of rush and bracken and coarse moss.

Sallow of cheek, a crow's wing
Of hair over the brow's smudged
Vellum; their legs all red and scarred
With brambles and the bites of flies,
They patch and mend and milk and bake,
Enduring the long ache
Of loneliness, till you return
At twilight, and enduring then
Your sullenness. A fairy would
Have left you, angry; these remain
Through frost and snowfall, wind and rain
To comfort you in your wide bed
With the limbs' warmth if not the heart's,
Bearing in their patient wombs
The future victims of the hills'
Intolerance of those who strive
To tell bravely upon that bare
Page their human and green story.

1955

44

Growing Up

When I was young and little
The hedgerows gave me shelter
And the bright grass crooked a finger
Round my toe...

But that was long ago
When I was a boy, busy among the bushes,
Prying for small treasure like a thrush,
Or in the woods, dawdling on soft foot,
A vague restlessness at the trees' roots;
Who am now a man caught in the cold violence
Of the wind wave breaking above the dyke,
A man unready for the bloody vista
In the next meadow where the stoat strikes.

1955

Midnight on the Farm

Morgan, stop your silly talk
Of ghosts and ghouls; don't be a fool, man;
You'll have me quaking in a minute,
Going on like that. There's nothing in it,
I know, but still the nights are lonely
In a hill farm, and on such diet
Of old tales men's shadows grow
Unruly in the fickle light
Of a wood fire, so shut up, or –
Shut up, I said. I can't stand
A word more.
              God! What was that?
Morgan, where are you? Speak, Morgan, speak.
Come on, now, Morgan; none of your tricks,
Trying to scare me. I know you're there.
The door's still shut, no wind has come
Colder than fear to take your place
At the red hearth; the naked moon
Still craves admission. I can see
You crouched there, Morgan... Morgan *bach*...
O God, too long! Should he come now,
Smirking out of that dark corner
To sip slyly the warm pool
Of light fawning about my feet,
My mind would break as the night breaks
In a storm of starry and shrill laughter.

1955

Not So

It is not all that far:
Two hundred miles from where you are.
Lift the receiver, dial the right
Number, you can hear the wind,
Hungry for the white flesh,
That has only the land's bone.
Generations have left those hills
Emptier than when they began
Embroidering with stone
The garments of the thin soil.

I could take you from house to house
That has only the grey thatch
Of cloud now for roof
Or memory of a garden
Where once the trees bore
Fruit sweeter than these,
Berried but with the small rain.
I will take you instead to the one
Tenanted still. Look! Listen!

'Yes, I am Pugh; I will speak now.
You think my struggle was with the soil
Only, that wind's variable moods
And the sharp rain alone were my worry?
Let us go back: there was a day
In the small school, a visitor came
To speak to us; "That's a bright lad"
He said after, "what about him?"
He stood talking to the headmaster,
Looking my way. A vision of streets
Paved with an ore that was more exciting

Than the gorse gold or the sun's yellow
Brushed my mind; and a day later
My father spoke, urging the cause
Of the glib city against the fields'
Silences in which he was shut
Since before birth.

                You think it was easy
To say no, to pull down the blind
On a view like that, to turn to the heart's
Safer investments in field and tree?
You see me standing, a young heir
To the birds' music and all the wealth
Of the earth's flowers, my name engraved
On each acre, the broad day fair
To bias me? It was a day
Frayed at the edges, too poor to beg
The coldest welcome. And yet I stayed.
Stayed for what? Could I sail better
Than any of the rest the barren breakers
Of the hill soil? The question irked me
Worse than flies in the hot fields
Or hail that sharpens a March wind.
The preacher spoke of the land's vocation
From the high pulpit, my neighbours yawned
In the seats beneath. I knew them there
For reasons similar to my own
Lack of one. I saw them cling
To wrecked farms that only the tractor
Could tow to port. We became a part
Of a prize crew to be paid off
At the town's bidding. Always I longed
To break the convoy, to go back –
Back to what? Was I bound once
In a lost childhood for destinations
Not of the flesh? Ah, you who take me,

Alone and dumb in the fields' tide
For the tall beacon by which to steer
Your own courses, remember how
My mind's compass windily veers
From point to point and is not true.'

1961

Question

One thing he said
I recall still:
Never, he said,
Never give in
Even to truth
That is made by men
For themselves, stand
Always alone.

Have I stood so,
Training my roots
Back on myself,
Rinsing, drenching
By sharp emetic
The mind of thought
That is not pure?

I have stood lonely,
But not alone.
The long antennae
Were always busy
Sifting the air;
The brain's small cells
Filled with honey
Of flowers not mine.

Under my flesh
The blood flowed back
By many channels,
None of them clean.

1961

Indoors

It was easier to come out with you
into the fields, where birds made no claim
on my poor knowledge and flowers grew
with no thought but to declare God.

Within I had the old problems
to cope with: turning from the Book's
comfortable words, I came face to face
with the proud priests and their intolerant look.

1962

The Meeting

He was looking at a flower,
Not with love, but looking at it;
His plough was stopped in the top corner
Of a field he had just roofed.

There was nothing to say that the wind,
Repeating in a tree the unrecorded
Facts of history, had reached further
Than the cold porches of his ear.

He was looking at a flower,
As an animal looks, wondering nothing
About the mystery of its growth.
And why should he? He had grown, too.

With less beauty? Who is to say?
There was a likeness in his eyes,
In both their tenancies of the air's
Quietness. You could have passed

On the hill road, unsuspecting
That blank encounter in space-time
Of two creatures, each with its load
Of meaning not to be set down.

1962

Hiker

He lies now with that fierce message
Stamped on his flesh, who yesterday was well
And walked obedient on the sunlit mountain
To the call of things apart from himself:
Freedom and nature with its wide sky,
And loneliness like a cool bandage
Laid on a heart the world had used
Ungently since he was last there.

Was he aware of the slow clouds
Gathering like thoughts in a mind
Less settled than the day seemed then?
He walked on with a strange trust
Unhurriedly to that last audience
With such power as had this to say.

1963

Brochure

And the guide book?
Too wordy;
Cut it down a bit, say:
An area of high land,
Longitude 3° W.
Ordovician.
The people with dark hair,
Small in the thigh,
A large proportion
Dolichocephalic.
English the prevailing speech,
With periods of Welsh,
Mostly on Sundays.
Imports, strontium in bulk;
Exports, H_2O, free.

1964

Exile

There was a small bay with corrugated
Surface, and so pleasant
The confectionery of its foam.
He came there, and sold all his books,
And made virtue of the emptiness
Of his purse; lived three long weeks
On a diet of provincial talk,
While the sun set ever more bloodily.

Prettiness drained from the girls' faces;
Their kisses became monotonous as salt
In the sea wind. By the end of the month
He would have given the orchestration
Of all the waves for one voice at its selling
Of newspapers in the gutters of Paris.

1964

Frontiers

A few names I remember,
A few figures, too:
Richard ap Hywel of Mostyn,
And a date, fourteen and four.
'I dwell with my own people.'
The sun softened the hills'
Harshness; the firebird sang
In the sky. It was as near
To freedom as we came.
Every stone in the building
Was taken from the side
Of a nation; every edict
Absolute and just;
The parliament conducted
In a language not yours.

1964

Work To Do

You want me to say
They were bored with it:
Life like a stubbed fag relit
Each day, because there was nothing
Better to do; that was the way
They were made – and I'm not going to.
Of course, they went out at dawn
And shut themselves in the cold room
Of the wind, and stayed there
Till late evening, and came home,
Not noticing the thin moon's
Mineral, nor the jewelry
Of the big stars. If a bird sang,
Their ear registered the notes
As a pool rain. What of it?
Their minds were deeper than a pool,
Warmer to sit by.
                              Tell me
What they will gain by being shown
Their images in your hard mirror's
Surface? Some must endure
Loneliness and the fang
Of the weather. Let sweat be their serum.

1964

Yesterday's Farm

I went up the long, broken road,
Unsure of the way
And so, slowly, in the small car,
Looking from side to side,
Examining the place.
It was poor country,
Most of the houses empty;
Failure's crop unstored in the barns;
The chimneys rusty.
I passed the chapel, marked on the map,
Without seeing it;
And kept on to the last farm,
Where the road pointed.

I dislike such an arrival
In the stunned peace of a stone yard:
The scatter of brown hens
And uproar of frenzied dogs;
The people who come out to see
And go in again,
Waiting for me to knock
With my improbable explanation
Of why I have come there at all.
No one goes walking in such hills;
But they know the way;
Direct me there with their shy smiles
And unshy bodies.
I examine one as she stands close:
There is a roundness of the figure
That is not bad; and the good teeth –
I shall remember this girl
After the first hours have passed,
And the boredom begins

In the dry grass by the lake;
I shall propose a situation
That is untrue to myself.
It is not girls like these
Are the daughters of Prytherch.
I imagined a long, mournful face,
Sallow of cheek;
A body I could feel tenderness for,
History cringing in her eyes;
And found, where the road ended
And poetry should have been on draught,
This old farm with the present
About its neck, and this girl
Without anything but the appeal
To the male in me and the promise
Of children, which, I suppose,
Are now mostly what the race needs.

1964

/

Half-past Five

The wind blows at half-past five.
There will never be that party again;
The visitors have returned home.
What can one make of one's life?
There is the green grass without a face;
There is the sky that reflects it.
What has become of the thrush
In the yew tree at half-past five
When I was a boy that used to sing?
Someone has stopped up the flow
Of its notes. I see it clearly
On its dark perch; its bill is open.
It needs a new kind of poet
To find the words for the song
That is so far down in the throat,
That is secondary to the rhythm
Of the traffic. At half-past five
There is no such thing as a place;
There is the mind only with its dryness.

1965

Two Versions of a Theme

I

You couldn't, I thought, ask for
A seedier crowd than these Welsh
People, men and women; in their
Cheap shoes and expensive
Hats, blowing their noses, shuffling
Their cold feet, listening between lulls
In the gossip to the minister
Praying, while the stiff corpse lay
In its coffin beyond the reach of
Such cant. I would have turned
Furiously from those lurid
Noses and blear eyes to my
Car, but that a low sound
Arrested me, a hymn tang-
Led in that misshapen
But human wood, that directly
Freed itself and became art,
Palpable beauty hovering over the
Bent heads, waiting to be
Owned by them, had they looked up.

II

So, having said it, what have you said?
Made intelligible noises;
Beaten about a small bush
With the bird flown.

You went to a funeral, the same old thing,
And were disgusted:
Bleary eyes, and bald heads, and the prayers
A collection of cant.

You were turning away – they began singing,
Effortless beauty,
Spiring as most art has spired
From soiled fountains.

You forgot the crowd, the flowerless manhood
In its rank garden;
Seeing only the way the hymn
Endeared itself

To more distant mourners, the Welsh hills.
For a long moment
The music became the poem, that became you.
It is quenched now.

1965

An Old Flame

I wait for her to get on
The bus at each stop, but
How can she forty years
Too late ever succeed
In catching it? I notice
Fields that have shrunk, hedges
Thinned out, the unmanageable
Refuse of the ponds. I
Admit failure to undo
The new houses knotted in
The loved grass, but not this
Failure of the heart to
Acclimatise to her hair's
Seasons. Looking around
At the passengers, I incur
The sharp burning of the thought's
Icicle: she could
Be here now unrecognised.

1966

Images

There is an unspoiledness there,
A cleanness;
Even the killing is done cleanly,
And the seasons are beautiful,
As human ones are not.
He leaves his footprints there,
And the trees are excited
As though he had just left.
One can spend one's time
By waters that still have retained
Something of his reflections.

But here there is a long way
To travel, and more than time
Is necessary to adjust
To his absence in persons
So bland. Consider a woman's
Enmity, her dispatch
Of rivals. I have seen the smile
She gives herself in the mirror
Of her conscience that can convert
The believer to cold stone.

1967

The Reader

The lawn is covered with bright grass;
Hungry birds gather there.
Their prey is difficult to detect
From here. Beyond them are the trees,
Cherries and birches; there must be a nest
In one of them to judge by the frequent
Intersection of the eye's beam.

The council have made a road
To run parallel with the lawn.
Children and dogs walk on it,
Stopping a moment at the gate
To look into this world I share
With Hume and Kant. Its emptiness
Deters them. I would like to go out

And talk to them; but what could I say
In praise of it? I must watch their gaze
Refracted, and their small hands slip
From the railings. Where the roadway ends
The fields begin, and the thing-in-itself
Is waiting to be known and loved.
And they would take me, if I could ask.

1967

The Return

It is over so quickly.
I have looked forward for many hours
To this return through the moorland,
Coming up England on a day of cloud,
Through the boredom of its landscape,
Through the irrelevance of its fagged
History. I have thought of the scholars
Of Glyndŵr, leaving their books
For this same journey, for the excitement
Of the border. These fierce ramparts
Westward have filled my horizon
All day, supposing defenders
Of a like fierceness.
                              It is true
That history going on as long
As ours creates an illusion
Of size, as the failure to grow
Does also. Yet given the time
And the will, – car, this is what you have done
To us now: there is no oppression
Like yours, that leaves our acres
Unguarded, but makes them sudden
And narrower than the heart had remembered.

1967

The Need

Oh, I know them: reputable men,
Makers of verse, scholars, lecturers,
But without power, ineffectual.
None of them will ever set a bomb
Alight or bring disaster
On England. I see them going
About their business, borrowing a glory
From the setting of the Welsh sun.

Vision they have and love, too,
Of a sort; but not the love
Of the land, cherishing it
With their body as a woman
Her child, with the unreasonableness
Of a woman and a man's strength.

1968

Song

Dirty river
Lumbering through Zaragoza
To a rusty guitar
Rattled by German fingers,

Where the girls come round
Wearing not silk mantillas
But jerseys and blue jeans,
And the jota collapses.

1968

Thoughts by the Sea

I don't know;
I think there'll always be some of these about,
The incorrigibly human
With their dogs and their fags and children,
Stared at by indolent gulls,
Unconscious of history;
Worrying over the burrs on the mind;
Getting their cars stuck in the soft sand,
Rescued by strangers;
Shaking of hands all round,
The consortium of fools...

The mushroom cloud, toppling on itself,
Collapses in dust.
The days pass
Without poetry, without art.
Somewhere from under an old dustbin lid
The thing crawls;
Another and another. In the sick silence
The smut and the crap re-begin.

1968

Aye, aye –

They were not much good,
Any of them: porters, farmers, signalmen.
I stayed seventeen years, learning only
How to be thankful for not being thankful
For differences.
                   While they lived I praised them
For outlasting with the help
Of the doctor their uses. When they died,
I treated them to the hard rain
Of my tears, not wanting them
To be thankless, who had been good for nothing.

1969

The Grave

I pass your grave
Daily; walk up and down
On it. I know that under
The bright grass there is nothing
But your dry bones. Prytherch,
They won't believe that this
Is the truth. Rumours start
Like hill fires; empty minds
Blow on them. Someone has seen
You at a meeting; somewhere
A bomb grumbles. Echoes
Reverberate in the heart's
Hollows. Durable
As a tree in history's
Landscape, you are renewed
By wishes, by foliage
Of young hopes...
                 It is the old
Failing, a skirmish seen
As a battle, victory turned
To a legend before it is won.

1969

Old Man

I know;
He is tormented in
This flame. There is an inner
Hunger he is
Aware of and can't meet.
Seeing how beautifully
The day dies, hearing the blackbird
Whistle, conscious of flowers
That are nameless, he would cry out,
If he could, utter a poetry
So savage the great books
Of your writers, Keats and Blake
And Shakespeare, would remain
Closed.
       I sense this in him,
The travail of strong feelings
Not to be born, messages
From the depths never to reach
An audience. He looks at me
In his anguish, toiling on
Up life's slope with the huge stone
Of a tongue he has been burdened with.

1969

Shame

This is the botched land,
The land of a few
Rifles and home-made bombs.
The men drill in the back-yard
Of the heart, march to a dead
Music. But the police come.
The one-eyed marksman, the
Commandant blowing
His toy bugle – the world
Laughs at them. But the law
Puts laughter away. Leviathan's
Hide twitches. It tells its hurt
To the court. The jury
Is outraged. Three more men
Will suffer an iron
Clemency. In the striped flag
On the tower there is the insolence
Of a poster advertising
A nation for sale.

1969

Some Place

In Wales we ride round
And around; the perimeter
Is alien, the centre
Too close. Somewhere
There must be an area
Of calm, pure, clean
Air for the spirit
To inhale. Seeking it
We ride round and
Around the prescribed
Highways in insured
Motors, meeting ourselves
In our children's
Unfriendly mirrors.

1969

Symbols

An introduction to
Welsh history – what
Out of its packed happenings shall
I select? Llywelyn's head
On its spear, that sightless
Lantern? A morning in Ceri:
The Archdeacon triumphant
Among the yews, the bishop
In flight? The sob of arrows
At Hyddgen? Morgan shaking
The words from the great tree of
Language? Rebecca's daughters
At play? Penderyn's body
Tolling above the dark
Pits?
    I choose that map
Of an old woman with England
Upon her back, weary of
Her lot, and punishing her children's
Rejection of the privilege of it.

1969

The Wisdom of Eliaser

Water proud now and much
water come soon long time
it is not rain Eliaser
he can always big month
March with plenty work
and belly after long cold
empty what this big wind
mean I tell you listen
when streams dry and earth
cracks open like old mouths
toothless and sheep blather
in the ffridd look you
stick all your slates on
with spit mortar and cow
shit anything your blind hand
can lift and lug homeward
much wood and faggots and
dry sticks and pile your grate
high and say amen amen
Duw but you make botch of it.

1969

Ynys Enlli

Is it a reminder?
Is this why the sea leaves it
Unsubmerged? Tirelessly it repeats
Itself or re-arranges
Its outlines. Under the grass
Are the choirs of dead men.

On mornings that are too cruel
To believe in, it gives itself
To its fasts, to the flagellations
Of spray; suffering also
The bleakness of the seal's stare.

Sorrowfully the spirit
Inspects it. Its one tree
Is the cross, that a saint's hand
Planted; a lavatory now
For the starlings that have their roost there.

1969

The Bank Clerk

It was not the shillings he heard,
But the clinking of the waves
In the gullies and rocks of
Pwll Du. Turning them over
To the customers at the counter
He offered them the rich change
Of his mind, the real coinage
Of language for their dry cheques.

Punctually in the evenings
At Pennard he returned to
The poem's sum, wrestling with it
For delight, but with the sea's
Care, that on the blank sand
Tots itself.
          Clerks, businessmen,
Grousers about the cost
Of a poet, he has balanced honourably
His accounts, but – what about you?

1970

Farm-hand

There was something you couldn't find
An answer to. The question perhaps
Was ill-phrased. Day by day
You went out into the same fields
Expecting – what?
          Millions of seeds,
Exploding in the usual way,
Greened your world. All about you
Life, that was too big to be lived
By the one flower, the one bird,
Put on its innumerable forms
That silenced you, even as they prompted
The huge query.
          You kept hoping,
Perhaps, for some trick of the light
To fix in an eternal moment
Of meaningfulness the separate shapes
That teemed there? I have seen you kneeling
In the wet furrows, as though you prayed,
Through the long silences, to the earth mother
For testimony. I have seen you raising
Your brute face as to a presence
In the bleak sky...
          Is it from without
The answer is to come? I get no nearer,
Seeking with as much patience within.

1970

Nobodies

No faces of all that rough crew
Come back to me. Was it they grew
Like vegetables in that place,
And had only the convenience of names
By courtesy? I number them all
In the darkness upon my bed:
The men and women with the lean farms
Like dirty labels about their necks.
But no face attaches itself
To a name ever, and their vague owners
Remain featureless in the fields
Not looking at me, so that I know
To christen them by their farms only,
Wrenched in pain from the hill's side.

They have returned, most of them, to the soil
They came from. Yes, it is true
Their names live, not on the surface
Of a stone merely, but in a book
And my own mind. Yet there are times
It seems almost they are the names
Of one person, bent like a tree
And labouring up a long slope
To a summit that is always in mist
And scaleable only in dream.

1970

Somebody

Within this world are the great oceans,
And on those oceans the dark smudge
Of continents and the green islands
With towns and cities, their stone sinews
Taut under the soft plumage
Of dust and smoke. And in those cities
Are streets full of people of many colours,
Laughing, sighing, whistling tunes
Of times and places that are not now.
And one I saw a moment ago,
Who tried to keep on his poor hearth
Of bone the fire from going out;
Who tried to grow to the full stature
His shadow attained on the hard wall.
And his hands were clenched and his feet sore;
His mind ached and his brow was charted
With care, and fear formed in his veins.
Yet he looked up and smiled, as he passed.

1970

Vocation

Mine is the good cause
If lost. I revolve still
Among persons, give them names,
Join, bury them.

One comes into the world
Like a violet, so soft
The unseeing eyes. I brush
Them with water, the Church's
Sublime dew. He grows tall,
Absent; but will return
Soon with his bride, asking
The favour of the candles
And music.

                    Always
They go, and always
The hole in the ground waits.
The stone pages go on
With their story. God, I
Tell them, will read this. Together
We mend the edges of
Our amens. The planes roar
In the sky. Science repeats
Its promises. Against times
That infect I offer my
Priceless inoculation.

1970

Chat

What's that you say?
No never. Well, just once...
Oh, in Paris or somewhere.
She was so pretty. Imagine
Yourself in an hotel
Dining-room; the tables engaged
All save yours. There comes in
A woman, young, soignée;
Looks around, summons the head
Waiter. They confer. He approaches:
Would Monsieur? I arise;
She is seated. Slowly the conversation
Develops. She is well-informed.
I incline; would she allow?
Good. Waiter, some more
Claret. Over the glass
Rim a momentary fencing
Of eyes. Touché, touché:
This is my own blood,
Rich as mahogany,
She is drinking. I present
A new guard: this evening
Mademoiselle no doubt
Is engaged? No! Then...?
She tosses her curls, dandles
A small smile: It
Is not far; we will
Walk. In the spring gardens
All the birds of the city
In song. I begin to speak
As a poet. Like a Beatrice
She listens. The Faubourg
Is left behind; the boulevard

Narrows. There is no
Birdsong now; my rhymes
Falter. But the body
Is all awake, struggling
With no will to escape
From the meshes she has drawn
About me. An alley
Arrests her. I look
At the dark door at the end
That is like the gravestone
Of Villon, of Baudelaire, blistered
With the laughter of the whores
Of Paris... What was that
That you said? Well, yes,
I was taken in, I suppose.

1971

Dimensions

The sea turns over
In its sleep. It dreams
Of ships, ports, empires
It will devour.

The child takes a shell,
Listens; is tuned in
To an immense world the sea
Knows nothing about.

1972

Now

it is the character
   a place can have to be
      under an afternoon sky

in spring with gorse
   rioting and the sea
      not far off with fields

where a man can wander
   at will thinking on
      his existence feeling its weight

lift as the lark's clockwork
   goes on and the experiments
      in the soil's laboratory

continue the sheep's skull
   in the deep pasture loses
      its grin and the mind

alights there as casually
   as a white butterfly
      does and goes its way

1972

Autobiography

The fall of a great house?
        I smile – bitterly?
                sadly?
                        wryly?
                                Anyhow but proudly.

Two people cast up
        on life's shore:
can't you see the emptiness
        of their pockets,
                and their small hearts
ready to burst with
                love? Say 'feeling',
                and the explosion
not loud.
        They come to
        in a lodging, make love
                in a rented bed.

And I am not present
                as yet.
Could it be said, then,
I am on my way, a nonentity
                with a destination?
What do they do
        waiting for me? They invent
        my name. I am born
to a concept, answering
to it with reluctance. I am
                wheeled through ignorance
                to a knowledge that is not
joy.

Nothing they have they own;
the borrowed furnishings of their minds
frays. I study to become the rat
            that will desert
            the foundering vessel
of their pride; but home
        is a long time sinking. All
        my life I must swim
out of the suction of its vortex.

1973

Inferno

I came down
into the body like Dante
with Virgil among the long

dead, but without
his protection. Ghosts
that approached had power

over me to distract, to
lead me away in useless
directions. Voices

were here of those punished
for their offences, but
not warning, urging me on

to the like. How huge
is the body; how far
one can wander from the way

back to the original
light of the spirit. The blood
is too easy a river

to cross, and once one
is over the path slopes
ever more steeply. The ordure

begins, the stench of those
who failed to return. In
increasing darkness and

cold I begin to forget
my purpose. To surface
is all; to crawl out

on some limb
of the body to watch
with unchristened eye

the light-winged
forms as they soar
on invisible thermals.

1973

Sonata in X

Allegro

Fire – the combustion
of gases in the dark places
of his being; this was the beginning
of havoc. God heated
the instruments with
which to extract meaning,
sweating over them his excess
ichor. The furnaces
roared; stars were struck
from an enormous anvil
in the sulphurous smithy
of his imagination. He worked
and sang to the accompaniment
of a huge music, himself the player
of it and its composer.

Andante

An aeon went by;
                the worlds
spun, slowed, as though the conductor
were tired.
                God rested
awhile, fell into a deep sleep,
                        dreamed.

                        A landscape appeared
before him, as empty as though
music had died and fire
had not been. He looked

at it through the window
of his own breath,
                    warming it
with desire, so that a dew
                        formed,
lichens took root, it
became a garden,
                    growing
where things had grown
                        before?

Yes, there was the tree
in the midst of it, and around
it, the shapes dancing.
                    He listened to them.

Scherzo

'Quick, hold my hand.'
        'Where are you?'
                    'Here. Who is it
                        called?' 'I, looking
                for you. I have
you now, and my...'
                        'Faster, faster!'
        'No, stop.' 'I can't;
we must keep

going.' 'I am a top
        on fire. That whip!
                Ah, how cool it was

                in the tree's shadow!'

                'When it was green.'

Adagio

He was asleep long,
    mesmerised by the reality
of the dream, the compulsion
    of the voices and dancing.
He became cold. A shadow
    stood up between him
and the garden; a frost fell.
Darkness arrived, swallowing
the figures, so that he woke
    with a great cry. And lo, the shadow
was that of his own finger,
    pointed at him in accusation.

1973

Hamlet

How does Hamlet differ from John Jones?
You smile. Easy, you imply,
remembering his daily pilgrimage
about the parish, from house to shop,
from pub to urinal; the sick reek
of tobacco; the village wind
sour with his talk. Not easy to forget
a man who for seventy
odd years sculptured his presence
in the drizzling workshop of the air
of Llanllyfni, his muscled oilskin
slippery in the neon-lighting
of the streets. You knew him, you
say; the grave's garrulous slate
proves he existed.
                But I didn't;
I must take your word for him.
It is Hamlet is real to me:
the pale prince on the perilous platform
of himself, a martyr to
thought; asking the question
of life that we all ask, and giving
us his shrill, indelible answer.

1974

Richard Hughes

He has gone now
to join his ship, too late
to board her. I remember
his beard, tangled
as his right mind
was not. I never got
to the bottom of him, but stuck
half-way down, clinging
to my preconceptions. Bald
brow, blue eye, watery
as a rainbow – his words
were dry spice seasoning
our nonsense. It was his trade,
sitting by the Welsh sea
forgetful of Branwen,
to use his pen for the incision
into the festering body
of Europe. There came out
the discharge of history
running gradually
clear for us in his precise prose.

1976

Where?

How shall we agree
there is evil, when no man
can put a finger on it?
I have cried: 'Lo here, lo there!'
and the landscape was empty.
If dead there were, they lay
under a far sky. I have wandered
the towns and the smiling secretaries
have received me. How could I hear
over such carpet the footsteps
of its approach? I have taken
hands and examined them
and they were as clean
as my own. I have looked
in the eyes of businessmen for the guilt
that was not there. I have tapped
the sincerity of the oratory
of the politicians and found their English
too good. Far up in the blue,
over the heads of a converted
people, I have seen nothing more dangerous
than their aircraft silently building
the rafters of the temple of peace.

1976

The Climber

Climbing mountains was climbing
himself. From the summit
he could look down and see below
the problems he had left behind.

Thoughts were like flowers on
the ledges, high up and far out,
the best needing to be plucked
dangerously and smelling of courage.

At night there was this mountain
above him, dark as the cave
of sleep he would enter and emerge
from tomorrow to resume his climbing.

1977

Dedication

He did it for the girl
he decided not to do it
with. Later generations
applauded the felicity
of one chosen for the denial
of his attentions; but for him
she would be wrapped in the anonymity
of the ashes of an urban
crematorium, tickling the nostrils
of the passers-by.
                But here she is
in indelible letters on
the inside page of the first edition
of his poetry: Jennifer James.

Who was she? The biographers
have it: the second daughter
of a small sweetshop-keeper
in the suburbs. But none have
her picture. We are left to imagine
the loveliness of one he would not
intrude on; heavy hair, skin
of a mistletoe whiteness, green
eyes – the mind dresses up
the plump, covered with freckles
body in its conventional
gingham that for a fortnight
or so he lusted after and veered
away from to the chastity of his verse.

1977

Pension

Love songs in old age
have an edge to them
like dry leaves. The tree
we planted shakes in the wind

of time. Our thoughts are birds
that sit in the boughs
and remember; we call
them down to the remains

of poetry. We sit
opposite one another
at table, parrying
our sharp looks with our blunt smiles.

1977

The Source

This is the journey that going back
on makes all things clearer
to the mind. I follow again the hymn
stanza by stanza to its beginning
in the imagination of Ann
Griffith and find it was the same source
that all drank from who took their departure
from God. There is a congestion at the fountain
that thins out as we go back
till it is only one who watches
the drops returning to it as leaves
to the tree. There are too many of us
now. In the deciduousness
of the nation it is hard to discover
pattern, but the further we go back
the shapelier on the horizon
the tree that is still in bud
with its poets and princes. We land
on a fresh shore at full tide
with the first pilgrims and see the waters that
have conspired to confuse their wake.

1977

Staying

I travelled, learned new ways
to deceive, smiling not
frowning; kept my lips supple
with lies; learned to digest
malice, knowing it tribute
to my success. Is the world
large? Are there areas uncharted
by the imagination? Never betray
your knowledge of them. Came here,
followed the river upward
to its beginning in the Welsh
moorland, prepared to analyse
its contents. Stared at the smooth pupil
of water that stared at me
back as absent-mindedly as a god
in contemplation of his own
navel. Felt the coldness
of unplumbed depths I should have
stayed here to fathom. Watched the running
away of the resources
of water to form those far
seas that men must endeavour
to navigate on their way home.

1977

Coming of Age

The repentances are over.
The prodigals have nowhere to return
to. They are their own
fathers and forgave themselves
at their setting forth. Did
they ask to be born? Their sperm
now makes no such demand
on the future, navigator
as it is of a dead
sea. If they walk with their heads
in the cloud, it is a nuclear
cloud, whose electricity is
the music they tune
their guitars to. They hold
hands in consummation of
a vow to acknowledge no
vow that we know, and look out
on the world with eyes that
are hard and bright and conscienceless
as the machinery they despise.

1978

Progressions

Time is that which is given us
to save and we save it at the expense
of spirit, and the boundaries
recede. There is a conversation
which we are not members of, which
we overhear; it is of echoes
answering echoes; it is as though
we were here all along, discoverers
of a revealed truth. Ah, the provincialism
of space, for beyond it and
around is that expanding
territory waiting to be colonised
by the thing-in-itself. It is the roles
we appeared in that invite us
to return, but always through rifts
in our vocabulary, in the intervals
between where we are, we stare
out at that unending journey
before us whose distance is what it means.

1978

Appointments

In their fifties, in their forties
some of them; the small ailments
for which there are now cures
carried them off. Were they conscious
their days were rationed? They took
wives, begot children, fiddled
in a local quartet. Did they sit
under a dwindling candle over
a dead book? Where did they get
their knowledge from? Were there servants
for that as there are now
computers? I think of Wordsworth
boiling his eggs, Coleridge wearing
his shoes out under a Stowey
moon. These had time, both
of them. What of the others,
those who 'in a short time fulfilled
long years'? Did Shelley between
long poems fit in his longer
travels? And what of Marlowe and Keats?
'A free man thinks of nothing less
than of death.' These drove their pen
daily under its lowering
sky. Were they, then, not free?
The distance between one place and
another was like time spent on their knees,
gathering treasure. Between one
hour and the next the cupped mind
did not upset itself, but remained
full, still and deep as the firmament
it reflected. We have shortened
our journeys but have nothing to do

with our time. Hurrying between
one place and the next we make our plans
of what we will do, when we have saved
enough of it to retire on.

1979

Cancellation

Out of his disinclination
for poetry of one
kind he made poetry
of another. Facility
of the pen with old
words, images from a time
that was past had continually
to be checked. The natural
world was his temptation,
providing the adjectives
that discredit. There was a
need for the inner landscape
of ideas, a place where the electrons
sang in the silence following on
the solution of an equation.
From too much weather whose epithets
were exhausted, he turned to the still
calm at the nucleic centre,
where art and science confronted
one another over the unsigned
truce that would minister to their estrangement.

1979

Codex

The old man takes pause.
Where is there to travel to
now with everywhere
discovered, Byzantium
in ruins? The desert
islands, whose palms
are umbrellas? The interior
journey? He yawns
over the familiar curios
on the mind's shelves. Jacob's
ladder: the Indian
rope trick of the soul? He
calls up and is undeceived
by his ventriloquism. Voltaire's
garden? He has over-cultivated
it already; the dust rises
in the hour-glass that is himself.

1979

Coming True

Not God, but a feeling of belonging
all places. The water at the Poles
circulates in us as the light does
from the Great Bear. We remember

the future as we anticipate
the past. We watch the weevil
at work as we do the hand
of a great sculptor. We are at home

with violence, but sallying
forth we find ourselves under
a serene sky. We fly our experiments
in the sun's face and the wax does

not melt. The universe is
our parish, and each of us
is his own church with an altar
waiting for the sacrifice of his superstition.

1979

Converse

You withdraw
        to where you are
and are near
                as you are far
off.
    We address you
in silence.
        You answer
us with the echo
        that never dies, that
is as though thought
        were haunted.
    We set
our ear to your
                presence
and the great shell
        of your being
throbs with the language
        that is as unknown
to us as it is
                familiar,
that is the communing
        at the centre of agitation
of the self with the self.

1979

General X

1

I was educated for war;
foretold it without excitement;
prosecuted it with excess of blood,
apologising to the future.

Who would not fight for his own acres?
Mine were the greenest in England,
as was my education in the fine
arts. It is the way one steps

down, whether out of a helicopter
or from an abandoned
standard of morality that
counts. The gloves off, I found there were no levels

to truth. The objectives justified
the methods. Survival was no cause
for congratulation. I deceived myself
with my promises, as I did not

them, and yet they thanked me for it.
Signatory to the savagery
indispensable for a just
peace I left others to draw the line.

2

'I want you to remember
the illegitimate children
for whom you fight; the
homes that were the false addresses

you gave. I want you to make
our capital sure it has men
to defend it. I stand
here in the casts-off

of Napoleon, fumbling
for the oratory appropriate
to all those of you who
received orders to volunteer.'

3

Came home no better
than I went out from the insouciance
of larks over the battle-
fields to the inclemency of the climate
of her pale eyes. Invented my memoirs
for the press; intimidated
the bench. Over the grouse
at table reminded them of the medals
I was not wearing. Stayed long
over the port, waiting for the reinforcements
of their laughter to fill up
the gaps in a story that,
like all stories of human
accomplishment, was being attacked in the rear.

1979

Quest

You are not the first to arise
and cry: Happiness is not
here; I will take ship and
pursue it over the world's waters.

It is a disease of time. Homer
knew it and drove Odysseus
seaward to sit in far palaces
remembering. Who said the Crusades

were for the release of Jerusalem
from Mohammed? They were to remind
men battling up Calvary's hill
of how far off they were from the Cross.

Columbus nudging his way west
was expositor of a new theory
of sound, that from such slight impact
as his the echoes will never be done.

So where you are, traveller,
is the best place, and inward not out
your journey through dark ante-rooms
of the species to where the self sits and waits.

1979

Sister Non

From all that silence and emptiness
　　　there was this to report:
that the god had been seen most days
　　　at the food-table, hungry for what
she could not provide, picking over
　　　her prayers. No meat! The wings lifted
and he was gone. A cloud passed, dragging
　　　what might have been his shadow
in its wake, so enormous
　　　its bulk. As there was time
there for the cartography of the lichen
　　　on stone, so there was time, too,
for her mind to embroider the air's
　　　cloth, fumbling for the pattern
that would reveal all: why she,
　　　the betrothed of God, was rejected
by him; why on the altar she
　　　had prepared there was only
the stone for bread and the rain's tastelessness
　　　to drink? On such sacrament as
this a saint would have sharpened
　　　his tongue. She smoothed hers
on it, running it over it as an animal
　　　does on what it has brought forth.

1979

113

Stop Press

All the papers carry it
in naked letters: God's bluff
called at last. The bedroom
with the words over the door:

Do not disturb – has been forced
by science and found to be
empty. Man celebrates the ending
of his tiptoe existence.

The world has become a window
of plain glass for more and more
people to press their faces against
laughing and crying: There is nothing there.

1979

Excursion

Went to the sea; stared
at the birds. Did they
stare back? Nature looks
through us, beyond
us, into a territory
always denied us. Held hands
with a prinked girl; showed
her what she showed
him, a featureless
interior. The gland
sagged. Emptied in the train
home, inaccurate
hour-glass, the sand
from his shoes. Peered
through a hurrying window
at the still fields
with a star over them
like life itself,
signalling meaning
to him on the one
wavelength he could not receive.

1981

Grass Platforms

Will they remember
    standing on grass platforms
the train coming in
    over the dusk fields
flying its smoke with the white owl
    drifting beside it?

Where has the guard gone
    in his buttercup braid?
Where are the signals'
    red and green flowers?
Who will remember
    the holidays that were spent
here, the voices blossoming
    in the sea wind? (Petals
now on a cold shore.)

                    Tunnels have swallowed
the last whistles. Sleepers under
    the wheels' spell
waken to an unprincely kiss.
                    Only the name,
    skeleton of an old language,
indicates to the casualty of time
    there are still places.

1981

The New Noah

Day by day loneliness,
emptiness, with nothing but the whales
rolling, sometimes too
near. He blessed them
but not in the old way;
he had the depth charges ready.

His aloneness increased.
The old human love was aflame in him.
A bird came winging
over the waste waters, settled
on the aft-hatch. He put out a
dry hand, but the bird clawed him.

He sent it forth
from his ark to search for the land
he longed for and must not
touch, to bring him a leaf
from a green tree. The bird returned
towards evening, but with blood on its bill.

1981

Predicaments

Do not go too far back.
Everyone who retraces
his thought finds somewhere
deep in the shade Plato
and Aristotle preparing
their ambush. What did they know
of the intellect's gestation
of the machine? Poems we threw up
too far back are not
to return to; they smell
sour. Yet fast as we push
on, we are outdistanced
by our conundrums. Rub Plato's
lamp and Malthus appears,
a genie of direr aspect
than an idea. It is not the vocabulary
breeds. Over-populated as we are
with our terms, it is things
that are fertile, the entities without
life, whose appetite is our undoing.

1981

The Tree

I speak of the tree in the mind,
its foliage our language.
The princes sat down
in its shadow, the light
sifting through, and planned
their campaigns. Seven centuries
later the English axe
at the roots is blunted
by our endurance.

                For the nourishing
of this tree, what the specific?
Some have their drops of blood,
a pipkin among the ocean
that is being shed. The veins of a small nation
are soon dry. Some identify
with the leaves, falling
in autumn to re-assemble
in their children. They can be picked off
one by one, so that the tree
dies.

        Do you ask me for an answer?
I have none. I know only
that the tree is ourselves, different
as the instruments of an orchestra
are different, but without which
the symphony is incomplete.
Our ancestors were the wood
the instrument is made of.
It is at our lips
now, and time pauses
a moment, waiting for us to breathe
into it with such breath as we have.

1981

The Big Preachers

Of atoms were ignorant and molecules;
but thundered verbally from their high
pulpits, ranting captains pacing
their unstable bridges and warning always
of the wreck of the soul. No scientist
had their renown; the invisible
was undiscovered. What was made
plain by the lightning flash
of their faces was the Creator's
inimitable purpose. And the people hungered
for more, exposing themselves Sunday
by Sunday to that tempestuous
weather, sharpening their appetite
thereby. You have heard the story
of the visiting preacher's drawing
of a pretended bow, and how they parted
for the shaft to go by? Those
were the imagination's heydays
and will not return. Being too thick
to give ground, we take our stand
now on the facts, and the facts
must do for us, a multitude at a time.

1983

Cybi and Seiriol

It was well
with him travelling
in the morning eastward,
in the evening

west. It showed
in his face; his countenance
was of a warm
hue. Was it well

with the other, leaning
over his own
thought, etiolating it
with his shadow?

They met in a clearing
at midday at an altar
of silence, crumbling
the light, pouring

the darkness, the
elements as necessary
to their celebration
as the bread and the wine.

1983

Feminine Gender

It has the elusiveness
of great art: the poem
so near, unwilling to be written.
I have knocked all these years
at the door of a supposed house
with somebody inside
(the movement of a curtain)
who refuses to answer.
                      Sometimes
as a face in chapel
it has appeared, raven-haired,
sallow of cheek, staring
through locked fingers. I waited
to have speech with it after
and it was gone.
              Mostly
it was the shadow of a bent
woman, too old to believe in, disfiguring
my sunlight.
              Was she ever
a young girl, as innocent
as compelling, before history submerged
her in the anonymity
of the valleys?
                Some must have known
her so, giving her a name
to live for, to die for, and a language
like seed corn, coming to harvest
again, as often as it is cut down.

1983

Poets' Meeting

Wordsworth was there, mountain-
                browed, and Shakespeare,
of course; Dunbar also;
Dafydd ap Gwilym, frowned on
                by the English.
There were Aeschylus, too,
Catullus and the time-quarried
face that had taken
Yeats' eye.
        Dunbar, swearing
at the thistles in his beard,
opened the discussion.
             The rest
blinked, until Wordsworth,
shining behind his thought's
                cloud
answered in iambics to set
Aeschylus booming.
           The consonants
clicked as ap Gwilym
countered, a turnstile
too fast for Catullus
to get through.

          Pray silence,
a voice crackled, Shakespeare
will speak now. And the others
desisted, looking amusedly down,
             each from his own slope,
on the foreshortened figure
            in honest kersey
poaching its dappled language
             without protocol on the plain.

1983

Repertory

Appearances are
    to be kept up;
it was for this Englishmen
    were created. 'Good luck,
Captain,' the Colonel
    says. 'See you
tomorrow.' Knowing he will not
    see him again. 'Thank
you, sir,' says the captain,
    'I'll look forward
to that,' knowing he is
    too forward. They keep the rules
with a straight face. It
    is the others who let
them down: the Irish, the
    winking Welsh. A door
opens in a parlour behind
    the coffin and there
in the kitchen are the tears and
    the whisky and the insincerity
of the black cloth. For the
    Welsh it is a play
nobody wrote, whose cast
    is the audience. For the
English it is one with three
    acts, so there is time
for performance. They hold their
    roles after the falling
of the last curtain lest
    it should rise as that door
opened and they should be caught
    fraternising with their reputations.

1983

The Undying

Needing no resurrection
they are alive in the pages
of our story: Glyndŵr
with his slow smile of disdain

at a time's subterfuge – too late,
indeed! And Rhodri o Fôn
sitting a little aside
with his men, refusing

to be drawn by the Arch-
bishop. It is our place still,
while the neighbouring nation
goes on its heretical

crusades after a retreating
glory. Ann, dear, when it was a time
for dancing, you danced.
When the bridegroom called to you,

you put off your shoes
and went as though over
divine ground, knowing
the tree he stood under

was the Welsh tree, not
borne down with his betrayed
body, but re-leafing itself
for joy with the words out of his mouth.

1983

The Cry

A cry. Who gave it?
     No one. It is the cry
of humanity, that unseen
creature that can do nothing
but suffer.
       I advance
to the poem's frontiers, where
the torturers and usurers
are more than proud of their grey
notice. Theirs is the underground
world, where under an obscene
acupuncture the prisoners
are cured of their allergy
to the truth.
       The revolver outpaces
the lancet, writing in prose
on the blank flesh.
       Show me
the engaged heart at the conference's
table, on the hot line, over
the wineglass at the reception
where handkerchiefs are brandished
       to remove from the eyes
tears of oil, lest someone should see
far down under the surface
the scaled monster in its primaeval slime.

1986

126

Caught

The Pale Clouded Yellow
      that is a buttercup
in flight, which I catch
and hold under your chin
asking you if you like
      now or always.
      And 'Certainly'

you reply, taking my hand
      in yours and prising
the fingers open to discover
      the butterfly, broken-winged.

1988

The View from Europe

And that was Africa:
the long line to the south
little higher than the Atlantic
that defined it. The sea rolled its drums
on the shore, broke in white
foam, flowers for the hair
of the girls. I sipped the wind
with my nostrils, and the smell
was the smell of fear. Two million-
year-old skulls surfaced
from soil fathoms, grinning
their disdain at the accuracy
of the new weapons. And that was Eden
indeed: Adam was black and the woman,
Eve, was black; and the serpent,
master of the click languages,
spoke to them sibilantly
of how the machine would sound
as it waited under the tree of death,
offering them nothing but a pretence of life.

1988

A Wish

Three fields, one
to produce, one
to lie fallow, one
to take my repose

in and, decontaminated,
to awake to the night-
conceived mushroom
stillborn in the dew.

1988

A1

Not signalling, picked up
all the same; in the back
with her, squashed together,
no need. Soft. In the look-back
mirror the husband's eyes
watching. I offer a
cigarette. In the dark
after the struck match whose
voice is it asks: 'How far
do you want to go?' As
though he had said: 'Lend me
a hand', I lend it, to her. It
is not refused. He steers
the car; she steers the
conversation. I prefer
her direction. But to arrive
is to stop, is to be
put out. 'She goes well,'
I remark, and the eyes
smile. Whose eyes? His in
the mirror, mine in hers,
hers to herself? He accelerates, she
relaxes. Whose is the next
move? I watch as the inns
fly. I could stand her
a drink; could I stand him,
too? I fondle the idea
of how, after a night with
her, his toast would be cold.

1989

Epilogue

Inside to a packed
theatre life
is being played, its failures
applauded. On the pavement

outside, after the coming
down of the curtain
on the last act mechanically
as a tear, it is there,

too, in imitation
of itself, boneless hands
grappling their pity. They brush
past, turning the collar

of their consciences up,
their responses at zero
at a noticeable lack
of artistry in the performance.

1989

Gwallter Mechain

He taught that God's kingdom
is within the seed,
and that sowing it carefully
should produce temples of corn
in which they could worship.

He preceded the machine.
Before pesticides, before
fertilisers, he expounded to them
the principle of growth,
the patience by which the good

should hold its own with evil.
He was contemporary also,
showing them how the kingdom
is new every year, the rotation of flesh
leading to ripeness of spirit.

He was big medicine,
too, to the artless
of mind, keeping the miscreant
all night on a stone
in the mistletoe river.
He was high up, as
they called it, the peasantry
perpendicularly glancing,
unable to scale him,
unable to discriminate
between learning and magic.
As did Nicodemus
before them, they came to him
by night, in the darkness

their minds cast. His was the thread
between elbow and finger,
measuring the sly length
between sickness and cure.

Y nos dywell yn distewi, – caddug
yn cuddio Eryri.
Yr haul yng ngwely'r heli,
a'r lloer yn ariannu'r lli.

The poor priest
of a dispensable parish,
dying intestate
to the world, but to us,
executors of his effects,
bequeather of the above
jewel to light Welsh
confidently on its way backward
to an impending future.

He took time off
to lecture to audiences
in the bird-deprived cities;
their applause died
away to the clapping of doves'
wings in the trees at home.

The weekly climb
into the crow's nest of his pulpit,
telling them of the glimpsed land,

trying to believe in it
himself. The words digested
the bell's notes more easily

133

than his intellect his doctrine.
Agriculturally he was way
out. Was he a reactionary

in religion? At the year's turn
he preached of the Janus-faced
God, of how the blood

on his threshold was berries
fallen from the dark tree of man
in disparagement of a whiteness.

1990

NOTE: The Welsh *englyn* incorporated into the text is by Gwallter Mechain (Walter Davies, 1761-1849, himself a former rector of Manafon, 1807-37), from his *Awdl ar Gwymp Llywelyn* (1821):

> The dark night becoming silent, – mist
> hiding Snowdonia.
> The sun set in its briny bed,
> and the moon silvering the sea.

Insularities

(for a nun on her island)

The automised light
reminds of a devotion
that is not automatic.

So many years now
praying to a god
white-headed as the sea

gesticulating at her window.
Rising in the small
hours, bruising belief

on the darkness, she crumbles,
her own ministrant, the dawn
on a depopulated altar.

She is her own tide, too,
Returning thirstily to a shore
littered with her Amens.

NEW MIDDLE EAST CRISIS.
(The unconscious irony
of the Press!) THE UNSTABLE
POUND PLUMMETS. (Trident surfaces
amid the tears of the poor.)
The news is washed up months
late on her unpunctual
island. Learned enough to have heard
of Nietzsche, she gives no sign
she remembers, finding God's

son new-born each day
on her surprised door-step. Bending
over him in her mourning
habit, with the clouds raftering
a Florentine sky, she is motherhood
interpreted by an earlier
master, with the beams slashing
it in surrealist disdain.

Hold hands;
round we go.
Mary is queen of – oh,
why did she do that,

breaking the ring,
sitting apart in
a place by herself?
We were only playing.

To the starer across
the water, no answer,
only the question:
reality or illusion?

A solitary neither
proves nor disproves God.
What we call narrowness
perhaps is vocation.

The scientist pores over
his glass, as she over
her soul's mirror. What
in a round world is

the criterion of their error?
Here on the main land
the ground is moving under
our feet. There, amid

baptismal currents, her faith
is as lichen, clinging
closely to a fabricated cross
that is contemporary always.

1990

Cymru (Wales)

Whose beauty was responsible
for your prostitution. Mournful lady
weeping in your waterfalls and streams,
birch-brown hair on the wind,
body lissom as the young ash,
in your morning or evening
dance casting your veils of mist
to reveal the boniness of your structure.
You have put on industry
like a shroud; made your face up
with oil and coal dust; announced
to the flourishers of cheque-books
you have your price. Forgive us
our failure to teach you the meaning
of true love, our readiness to watch
you soliciting, not for us to have
bread to eat, but for burying
under the excrement of factories
the clover that sprang where your foot fell.

1991

138

Wings

Six years of war that
no treaty has ended.
The sea's barbed wire
on the beach tonight
glitters with the moon's blood.
The waves' artillery
is the inevitable rumour
of ravages to come.
                                    I have
no tower, only a cottage
to proclaim a warning
of the barbarism at hand.
The bees have gone from mankind's
tree and only wasps
nest at its roots, producing
no honey. I have not lived
with nature so long
as to be blind to its symbols:
the comb's structure, a miracle
of design, has become a hangar
for the striped bodies, swarming
upon the ripe fruit, drowning in it
and stinging the hand that would help.

1992

Process

Not satisfied with
the fairness of nature
they began imagining
the fair city: buildings
to sail the horizons;
deciduous fountains always
renewed; the inhabitants also
with foreheads unclouded.
The fields would come up
to its walls, lapping
at them, always in check.
No necessity for
legislation, the laws pressed
in their hearts as petals
between the pages of an old book.
A dreaming populace
to inhabit its walls,
arguing far into the
night over the priorities
of the beautiful and the true.

The city arrived.
Quis custodes custodiet?
It was because the good
hung back that the government
passed into the iron
hands of the single
of mind, the double talkers.

1993

Sick Child

We prayed hard;
we believed true.
All I remember
is fair hair, blue
eyes, looking at us
without seeing.

We held hands.
He remained dumb,
the would-be conductor.
Faith's alternating
current was switched on.
We buried her smiling.

1993

141

Born Lost

It is a thicket;
the branches are bone.
Faces stare out at us,
human faces with mouths
wrenched on a wild cry:
'I am hungry, I am
alone.' To be born
lost – what greater misery
can befall? They offer
their plight and we nod
as we pass, dusting
them off our coat sleeves.
A coin is no key
to their enclosure, so why
waste one? The mind sheers
off the difficulty
they present: 'Neither this man
sinned, nor his parents...'
Who, then? Where did the road
fork, and who threw the genes'
dice? There is no answer
but that we are committed
to pursue it, they
with their mouths open,
we with the minds that
love grudges us closed.

1995

The Lesson

The bird man explains
how the male bird has to establish
territory, advertising, by singing,
his presence. (Have you heard God
sing?) He demonstrates
how where you had thought
there was nothing a bird
crouches. (Protective camouflage?)
There is not one bird but thousands
and thousands of species, each
separable by its feathers.
The comparison fails
here. Life, it is true, has its feathers,
but they are not all part of the plumage
of the one God. (Perhaps history
has its nights, when that God
roosts with his head hidden.)
No matter, they are alike, these two,
in migratory behaviour.
One day the hedges are alive
with hurrying bodies as a mind
is with thoughts. On the morrow
they are deserted, another country
becomes jubilant with bird notes.
Where has God gone? The mind's branches
are empty and without
song. Their leaves are encrusted
with town dust. Return, migrant,
so your listeners arising
on some May morning of the spirit
may hear you whistling again
softly but more musically than any of their inventions.

1995

143

Plas yn Rhiw

This garden is reflected
in an underwater garden.
When summer arrives
the wrack has the smell
of the bitterest of flowers
but domesticated by sunlight.

The tones of the old ladies
are sea voices lingering
in a shell. Roses hang
their heads as their presences
pass by; but pansies lift theirs
with velvet in their expression.

Between Irish yews
the air is a window
upon a Welsh sea
often dishevelled, although
not today, where distant
mountains vie with it in blueness.

The house, though old, reposes
on an earlier foundation,
sunning itself on the hill's side.
The wind in the rafters
at night is as an echo
of the conversation of princes.

It has been reclaimed,
delivered out of the clutches
of dandelion and ivy,
taken in care. Yet there is an ache
here the many contributions
of visitors can never assuage.

1995

A Species

It is a crackling of song's twigs,
but dry like the brittle
but bitter laughter of a young girl
at a tart joke; the scratching
of a match on a bare hearth,
an attempt to get April going
before February has departed.
It is a symbol of our condition,
a species parochial and important,
erecting our small edifices
in the context of space-time,
domesticating the wildernesses
that geology has bequeathed us.
Its nest is a twigged hovel,
illuminated by jewels.
Those blue caskets exhibit, when opened,
the contents that are their programme.
Their phrases, such as they are,
were not listened to by emperor or clown.
It is free will that is our problem.
In the absence of such wings
as were denied us we insist
on inheriting others from the machine.
The eggs that we incubate bring forth
in addition to saints monsters,
the featherless brood whose one thing
in common with dunnocks is
that they do not migrate. We are fascinated
by evil; almost you could say
it is the plumage we acquire
by natural selection. There is a contradiction
here. Generally subdued feathers
in birds are compensated for

by luxuriant song. Not so these
whose frayed notes go with their plain clothes.
It is we who, gaudy as jays,
make cacophonous music under an eggshell sky.

1995

Abaty Cwm Hir

The map lies, leading
    the visitor to Abbey
Cwm Hir, to the village
    post office with its jars
of dead sweets and anaesthetising
    staleness. The eye
is a bluebottle, flitting
    and alighting at last
on the official sign
    over the counter, the shotgun
marriage of English and Welsh.
    Nothing occurs here
except the continual rotting
    of a nation, rancid
with newsprint. Tell me
    isn't there another place
close by with a grave
    and a body in it,
whose nails are still growing,
    whose hair is the grass,
that is a stranger to corruption,
    that gives off a smell
as time-worn as cynghanedd,
    but with all the urgency of April?

1996

Calling

'Are you still there?'
I called out to
the beloved country.
The beams answered from
the island lighthouses
but there was no one there.
The ships entered our harbours
like shadows upon a screen.
In imitation of images
upon another screen
our people were brought up
to be grateful.
The coal dust was blown away
by the subsidised breathing
of the unemployed. Our villages
were museums to be entered
only if one could pay.
What was a green peace
was only an interval
in the coming and going
of jet aircraft practising
for war. My asking
was the repetition
of a question centuries
old, always in terror for fear
of a negative reply. I asked
it again this morning,
and like mushrooms
sprung up after a dark
night came upon
two children, their heads
together, the Welsh fresh
as dew on their lips.

1996

Elders

They are as rainbows
refracted a moment
in the waves breaking
at Aberystwyth: Gwenallt,
that man on wheels, to
and fro between study
and promenade, hurrying
in the wake of a receding
answer. Alwyn, back turned
to the best the ocean
could offer; mariner
among the nation's trickier
currents, battered about
by them, but like them able
continually to surprise. Saunders,
too small for his clothes,
too big for the strait-jacket
of our ideas; a cloud
on the horizon of the well-
to-do, but for those rich
only in the imagination
penumbra of an eclipsed
glory about strikingly to re-appear.

1996

Filming

'Strange,' she says,
'no photograph
of the Holy Ghost.'
I smile
and my smile
is the reflection of sunlight
in a mirror
lying about the parlour
quieter than water.
Would it were so
always. There are times
when I weep, pointing my lens
inward, so the old
human cataract intervenes,
blurring the true
film. It is then I see,
no matter how holy,
the ghost is a haunting
of self by the self;
that what sleeps
in the seed can erupt
outward till the whole universe
is a shape writhing,
its hair on fire
as a mind with thought.

1996

The Gallery

Friends? I never had any.
Acquaintances? Two or three.
My intimacy was with
the past. I was caretaker
of a gallery of dead
heroes, who had never had
their likenesses taken:
Llywarch Hen singing
the first bars of the
perennial lamentation
of our people. Owain Glyndŵr
scowling at the abbot
accusing him of having
over-slept. The Puritan
before his time, Siôn Cent,
pointing austerely at the coffin
in the chancel, shaking
a finger at the bird music
outside. Goronwy Owen,
not first of our exiles,
but epitome of all those
of our race whose destiny
was to hunger through memory's
prison bars for the sacrament
of our country. And finally he,
the small man with the big
heart, whom I met once
in our pretending capital,
taking my hand in both
his and soothing my quarrel
with my English muse with:
'But all art is born out of tension.'

1996

In Memory of James and Frances Williams

(founders of the first lifeboat in Ynys Môn)

The sea's tumbling escalator
beside them, they had a nickname

for the operator of it,
Davy Jones – an effort to domesticate

a monster. They peered
into his locker and saw bodies

like weeds dancing the dance
of the long dead. They leaned

from the bucking row-boat
to extend a hand to the living,

and so an association was formed
that was to rescue its thousands.

What can a stone say?
The only creases
on its forehead are
the lines of blurred print

the weather is erasing.
'In memory of' – the churchyards
are far off, yet this
is the headstone over

a myriad graves. To what
end this expenditure
of good granite? The sea
smiles and is never

to be trusted. Steam
has drawn the teeth
of the snags and skerries,
and the light drops only

a stone tear for the broken
masts and the torn sails.
But the gulls remember
the crews' wailing, and far

from the shore, as though
hands were lifted, the waving
goes on from casualties
surfacing for the last time.

Light steers to safety.
It steered in warped
hands vessels on the rocks.
Yet courage is that
which the good and evil
possess in common.
It was indiscriminate here;
the wreckers' relations
manned the first of
the life-boats. Grips had to be
prised from intolerable
oar-handles; and the Church
was there, putting prayer
into action, wringing from heretical
rollers a reluctant Amen.

We are mastering the planet.
The tide's pendulum is that
of a stopped clock where
hazardry is concerned. High

over precipitous breakers
the planes fly, ironing them
smooth. The brave answer
of the coxwain: 'We need

not come back, but we have
to go out' has shrunk
to a whisper. Put your ear
to this stone, so you may hear it still.

1996

Oil

Time has left open
its book of sand
for the aeroplanes
to study. At that height
all earth's mysteries
are made clear, only
the Sphinx's question
remaining unanswered
because it is unheard.
Yet huskily the bones,
the wind sawing at them,
make their reply: 'No
road here; either you
fly, or you perish; among
all these desiccated
fountains even the camels
are thirsty.' What, then,
a huddle of shadows,
are the Bedouin bent over?
Their scowls are for strangers,
the prophet's uncircumcised ones,
using those bones to divine
not water the soul
sickens without, so much as
that other mineral,
smelling of corruption, of which
the whole world thinks itself in need.

1996

Story

They had come all that way –
for what? There was no message,
there were no instructions
as to how they should face
the eternal indifference
of their surroundings. Upon the table
there was a key, mocking them
with an ability to lock
themselves in without locking
the enveloping emptiness
out. They stared at it
in the threateningly still
dusk. Was it a symbol,
a key to the meaning
of their existence? The men left
one after one, the provisions
with them. A month later
those coming to relieve them
found only the stench
that lingers in hope's wake
and an expression on two
faces as of those who have seen
truth dawn, where there is no light.

1996

Tourney

Even now from a stone tower
I look east, look west, north and south
and see how the world, as the light shines,
shows itself to be good, bad, just or indifferent.
If the sun wakes me soon after dawn
with its pitiless candour, it is the moon
at last, with fingers to its lips, convinces
me that nothing is what it seems.

It was not long ago a horseman rode up
and blew on his gold horn, and my tower
still stood. Who is it now, master
of electronics, drives by and with one blast
summons me to unequal combat?
Lord of my life, tell me what armour to put on.

1996

The Hummingbird Never Came

We waited
breath held looks aimed,
the garden as tempting
as ever. Was there a lack
of nectar within us?

God, too? We
are waiting. Is it
for the same reason
he delays? Sourness,
the intellect's

dried-up comb? Dust
where there should be
pollen? Come, Lord;
though our heads hang
the bird's rainbow is above us.

1997

Pharpar

Rivers are for bringing
a woman's sweetheart to.

How often she has walked
by one's side, seeing her life

running away unaccompanied.
How often one has addressed

her in tones she wished
to hear only from the beloved.

It is a rippling body
reminding of embraces that she desires.

She sings to it in the hope
of being overheard by the one

who is far off, watching herself
change in its unchanging mirror.

1997

Blackbird

Its eye a dark pool
in which Sirius glitters
and never goes out.
Its melody husky
as though with suppressed tears.
Its bill is the gold
one quarries for amid
evening shadows. Do not despair
at the stars' distance. Listening
to blackbird music is
to bridge in a moment chasms
of space-time, is to know
that beyond the silence
which terrified Pascal
there is a presence
whose language
is not our language, but who has chosen
with peculiar charity the feathered
creatures to convey the austerity
of his thought in song.

1998

Diary

On Monday a stricken
faith on his doorstep, bleeding

from Sunday's wounds. On
Tuesday love's garbage

bins empty. The shadow
of time already fallen

across Wednesday. On Thursday
a journey undertaken

without hope while carpenters
rough-hewed the cross

we would hang Friday's
credulity on. On Saturday

aha, on Saturday he was at
the races, where the machine

came hurtling in first
and was never the winner.

1998

Dreams

The poet sleeps,
his head on vocabulary's
stone pillow. How terrible
is that place, where angels trip it
on the dictionary's ladder
and only man is left
wrestling with his dream
of the great poem that refuses
its name. How the words
kept themselves in hand,
leading him on to this
final encounter with the themes
which defeat him. Here truth
tears the mask from its face
and his pen crumples before it.
Here love, its hand to its side,
watches as the woman passes
and he is not Dante.
Here beauty puts on its new clothes
for the dance with the machine
and he is blinded by silence
where he had foreseen din.
And here the dream changes
to nightmare, when the words
that had been Eden's chorus
become signs and equations,
and God leers out of the nuclear
cloud to imply how it is for this, too,
he has been waiting from the beginning.

1998

Everywhere

I had never been there before,
nor maybe had anyone else,
though the ring contradicted,
remembering the long oars
and the galleys like shadows
that came with the rising sun
and the frost on their armour.

What was the song from the rocks,
grey seals or the carolling of mermaids?
I had believed anything
in the half light with the great sea-horses
straining at their bridles.
God was never in charge here,
I repeated, eyeing the wrinkles

in worn cheeks too old to be human.
Yet why, if there were no God,
had I been brought there? To discover
him in silence or rather in his absence?
Suddenly I understood: the heaving
of the water was himself breathing.
The age was to remind how young

was a presence that had been there
for ever. I realised the wideness
of the sky was his face gazing;
that the curvature of ocean
was the emblem of a mind
rounded like space yet always expanding,
so the keeled stars could navigate him for ever.

1998

163

Island Boatman

That they should be braille
to him on blind days
of fog or of drizzle
he learned them by heart,
murmuring them over:
Pen Cristin, Briw Gerrig,
Ogof y Morlas, I listened
to them and they were music
of a marine world
where everybody wore ermine.

Was he religious?
He was member of an old
congregation the white-
surpliced island ministered
to, warning of the crossing
to a smiling Aberdaron
with tides at the spring.

Sitting with him over
a fire of salt wood,
spitting and purring, I
forgave him his clichés,
his attempt to live up
to his eyes' knowingness.
They had looked down so many
times without flinching
into a glass coffin
at the shipwreck of such
bones as might have been his.

1998

Talk

If words' purpose
is to conceal thought

our conversation served only
to keep meaning at bay.

Far into the night
over a sinking fire

we were as a murmur
of wind in the centuries'

chimney. One ran rings
round us with his pipe's

smoke though overrunning
himself in the end.

One was a listener
but had the look of one

being addressed from far off.
We imagined we played

Plato's symposium
over again, but Diotima

was absent. This
was male talk, gruffly

trying to grow wisdom's
moustache, yet failing

in the end so much as
to split truth's single hair.

1998

'Waiting for the tale to begin'

Waiting for the tale to begin,
not knowing that we are the tale,
that it began with us
and that with us it will end.
There was many a false start
but always the electrons were busy,
that dance in which to perish
was to survive in a different orbit.
We asked our questions and passed
on. The answer, discovered
by others, was to a different question.
Yet they, too, had the feeling
of having been here before.
We are our own ghosts, haunting
and haunted. We live out a dream,
unable to equate the face
with the owner, the voice
with the speaker, the singer
with the song. Ah, how we thought
science would deliver us, when
all it has done is to set us
circling a little more swiftly
about a self that is an echo.

2000

Birthday

Come to me a moment, stand,
Ageing yet lovely still,
At my side, let me tell you that,
With the clouds massing for attack
And the wind worrying the leaves
From the branches and the blood seeping
Thin and slow through the ventricles
Of the heart, I regret less,
Looking back on the poem's
Weakness, the failure of the mind
To be clever than of the heart
To deserve you as you showed how.

2002

The Father Dies

Ah, forget this snivel, the gone
lip. I am not maudlin;
it is just that all my life
I tried to keep love from bursting
its banks. Love is the fine thing
but destructive. I strove to contain it,
to picture it as the river
we lived by. But to fall
headlong in, to be carried away
in front of you, son; to have
no firm ground: a father drowning
in tears and without
breath to keep his voice casual
as in the old days; and the smile
you hold out to me breaks
like a stick, because there is
as much pity in it as love.

2002

Luminary

My luminary,
my morning and evening
star. My light at noon
when there is no sun
and the sky lowers. My balance
of joy in a world
that has gone off joy's
standard. Yours the face
that young I recognised
as though I had known you
of old. Come, my eyes
said, out into the morning
of a world whose dew
waits for your footprint.
Before a green altar
with the thrush for priest
I took those gossamer
vows that neither the Church
could stale nor the Machine
tarnish, that with the years
have grown hard as flint,
lighter than platinum
on our ringless fingers.

2002

The Hill

The hill is a skull that contains
many skulls. I am here now
to do their listening for them.
I hear what they did not hear:
the loud express rattling westward,
the more continuous undertone
of the car, a church clock registering
time in ways we have agreed to.
But there is one sound that is still
with us: the rusty machinery
of the stone curlew that was
before Christ that they listened to
over a cold hearth over a child dead
in its cradle and took no solace from.

2003

In Memory of Ted Hughes

I think looking askance
into nature's mirror he saw,
even as I do, a god
hiding his face. In answer

to the question 'where
does the blood come from?'
he imagined some iron
smithy, where drops were forged

to make nails for a defenceless
body, and pain shone its rainbow
through the sunniest of showers.
If birds sang it was out

of the depths of the crow's
shadow, and life in search
of what life is looked long
into its own entrails. Is there

mercy? He bends now
over a darker river, making
his cast times out of mind,
for the big poem, bigger than the last.

2007

'The computer is unable'

The computer is unable
to find God: no code
number, no address.
Technology stalls
without the material
we provide it. There must be
some other way. 'Try
looking' says the eye,
'Try listening' the ear
answers. I stare into distance:
nothing but the gantries
where art is crucified in
the cause of new art.
I have heard amid uproar
in London the black redstart
singing among the ruins;
so I strain now amid
the times' hubbub for fear
the still, small voice should
escape me. 'Is he dumb?'
Wrong language. 'Am I
impatient?' I resort once
again to the word processor.
But where a poem in his honour
should emerge, all in bud
like a birch tree, there is only
the machine's repetitions,
parallel tramlines of prose
never to come together in praise.

2008

'Easter. I approach'

Easter. I approach
the years' empty tomb.
What has time done with
itself? Is the news worth
the communicating? The word's
loincloth can remember
little. A thin, cold wind
blows from beyond the abysm
that I gawp into. But supposing
there were bones; the darkness
illuminated like a museum?
In glass cases I have
peered at the brittle bundles,
exonerating my conscience
with mortality's tears.
But here, true to my name,
I have nothing to hold on
to, an absence so much richer
than a presence, offering
instead of the skull's
leer an impalpable possibility
for faith's fingertips to explore.

2009

'One drop of blood'

One drop of blood
fallen from a figure on a cross.

One tear refrigerated
on the worn cheek of time.

One flake of snow
homeless under an overcast mind.

One feather torn
by the peregrine from the dove's breast.

One crumb of bread
in the smudged palm dazzling me.

2009

'A bird's prayer'

A bird's prayer is its song,
addressed to nobody
but the unknown listener
to its feathered vernacular.

Man's prayer is a trickle
of language gathering to a reservoir
to be drawn on by the thirsting
mind in its need for meaning.

2010

'Language has run its course'

Language has run its course.
After that first word,
that acorn that grew
to an immense oak tree
in time's forest, the leaves have begun
falling faster and faster
on the human garden,
where science's breath
lies on them like frost.
'But why despair?' technology
cries. 'Look, it is Christmas
again', hanging the bare boughs
with its baubles: telephones,
videos, computers, all those gifts
that make the threadbare
stocking of our humanity
bulge. I explore them
as once men must have
explored the wounds in the body
that hung on this same
tree, opening in them
the great flowers of our language,
whereas now, anaemically,
it is my own fingers that bleed.

2010

The Orphan

There is a small boy
in us that we exclude
from the pitiless surfaces
of the mirrors that life
would hold to him.
                    Grow
up, is what time says
to us, and externally
we obey it. The brow furrows
the mouth sets, the eyes
that were made for the reflection
of first love have a hole
at the centre through which
we may look down into the abyss
of meaning. But there is that crying
within of the young child
who has fallen and will not
pick itself up and is
unconsoled, knowing there
is nobody for it to run to.

Undated (post 1971)

Pact

This is my child;
that is yours. Let
peace be between them
when they grow up.

They are far off
now; let it not
be through war they are brought
near. Their languages

are different. Let them both
learn it is peace
in the hand is the translation
of peace in the mind.

Undated (?1980s)

BIBLIOGRAPHY

The following bibliography contains all of the uncollected poems by R.S. Thomas that we have been able to identify. An asterisk indicates a poem not included in the present volume.

1939

'The Bat', *Dublin Magazine*, 14.3 (July–September 1939): 8.

* 'Fragment', *The New English Weekly*, 13 July 1939: 204.

['I never thought'] [A typescript of this poem was collected in *Spindrift*, RST's unpublished first volume (late 1930s). The poem was first published in Byron Rogers, *The Man Who Went into the West* (London: Aurum, 2006): 53.]

1940

* 'Birches', *Dublin Magazine*, 15.3 (July–September 1940): 6.

* ['I know no clouds'], *Dublin Magazine*, 15.3 (July–September 1940): 6.

'July 5 1940', *Ringless Fingers* (Bangkapi: Frangipani Press, 2002): n.p. [A typescript of this poem was collected in *Spindrift*.]

* ['Look, look at the sky'], *Dublin Magazine*, 15.3 (July–September 1940): 6.

1943

'Confessions of an Anglo-Welshman', *Wales*, 2 (1943): 49.

* 'A Farmer', *Wales*, 2 (1943): 48.

1944

'Gideon Pugh', *Wales*, 4.6 (1944): 47.

1948

* 'Hill Farmer', *Wales*, 8.29 (1948): 511.

'Llanddewi Brefi', *Wales*, 8.29 (1948): 521.

'Song' ['Up in the high field's silence'], *Dublin Magazine*, 23.1 (January–March 1948): 3–4.

1949

'Lines for Taliesin', *The Welsh Nation*, 18.3 (March 1949): 5.

'Three Countries', *Dublin Magazine*, 24.2 (1949): 5.

'Welsh Shepherd', *Dublin Magazine*, 24.4 (1949): 5.

1950

'Y Gwladwr', *Y Fflam*, 9 (Awst [August] 1950): 42.

'The Two Sisters', *Welsh Nation*, 19.3 (1950): 1.

1953

'Auguries', *The Listener*, 15 October 1953: 632.

'Darlington', *Rann*, 19 (1953): 17–18.

'No Answer', *Dublin Magazine*, 29.2 (1953): 10–11.

'Peasant Girl Weeping', *The Listener*, 9 July 1953: 67.

1954

'Original Sin', *Dublin Magazine*, 30.2 (1954): 9.

'Proportions', *Dublin Magazine*, 30.2 (1954): 9.

'Somersby Brook', *Times Literary Supplement*, 13 August 1954: 518.

'A Welsh Ballad Singer', *Encounter*, 3.6 (1954): 64.

1955

'Commission: *for Raymond Garlick*', *Dock Leaves*, 6.17 (Summer 1955): 17.

'Farm Wives', *Dublin Magazine*, 30.4 (1955): 1-2.

'Growing Up', *New Statesman*, 12 March 1955: 361.

'Midnight on the Farm', *Dublin Magazine*, 31.2 (1955): 4–5.

1957

* 'History of a Race', *Dublin Magazine*, 32.4 (1957): 5–6.

1958

* 'Anthology', *Poetry Book Society Bulletin*, 19 (1958): n.p.

* 'A Blackbird Singing', *Listen*, 2.4 (1958): 2.

* 'Villanelle', Commissioned for broadcast on the Welsh Home Service,
  'Literary Magazine', 22 January 1958.

1960

* 'From Home', *Western Mail*, 20 August 1960: 5.

* 'Two Figures', *Times Literary Supplement*, 1 April 1960: 214.

1961

'Not So', *Poetry at the Mermaid* (1961): 64–5.

'Question', *New Statesman*, 29 September 1961: 434.

1962

'Indoors', *Poetry*, 100.2 (1962): 80.

* 'In Town', *The Listener*, 29 March 1962: 561.

'The Meeting', *English Poetry Now: Critical Quarterly Poetry Supplement*, 3
  (1962): 4–5.

* 'No', *Poetry*, 100.2 (1962): 82.

* 'To Church', *Poetry*, 100.2 (1962): 81–2.
* 'The Visitors', *Encounter*, 18.2 (1962): 80.

1963

* 'Eh?', *PEN* (1963): 123.
'Hiker', *Yorkshire Post*, 16 February 1963: 8.

1964

'Brochure', *University of Wales Review*, Summer 1964: 26.
'Exile', *Critical Quarterly*, 6.3 (1964): 212.
* 'Fact', *Forethought*, [Eton College] (1964): 37.
'Frontiers', *University of Wales Review*, Summer 1964: 26.
* 'Vagrant', *Perseus*, 1 (1964): 54.
'Work To Do', *Critical Quarterly*, 6.3 (1964): 212.
'Yesterday's Farm', *The Listener*, 17 December 1964: 977.

1965

* 'Ceridwen', *Transatlantic Review*, 18 (1965): 78.
'Half-past Five', *Transatlantic Review*, 18 (1965): 78.
'Two Versions of a Theme', *Agenda*, 4.1 (April/May 1965): 18–19.

1966

'An Old Flame', *Agenda*, 4.5/6 (Autumn 1966): 33.

1967

'Images', *Dublin Magazine*, 6.3/4 (1967): 38–9.
'The Reader', *Anglo-Welsh Review*, 16.37 (1967): 8.
'The Return', *Welsh Voices*, ed. Bryn Griffiths (London: Dent, 1967): 68.

1968

'The Need', *Poetry Wales*, 4.1 (1968): n.p.
'Song' ['Dirty river'], *Fishpaste Hors-série*, 3 (Oxford, 1968) [postcard poem].
'Thoughts by the Sea', *Clw* [College of Librarianship, Aberystwyth], 3.1 (Summer 1968): 9.

1969

'Aye, aye –', *Poems '69*, ed. John Stuart Williams (Llandysul: Gomer, 1969): 75.
'The Grave', *Anglo-Welsh Review*, 18.41 (1969): 16.
* 'The Lane', *Critical Quarterly*, 11.1 (1969): 6.
'Old Man', *English*, 18.100 (1969): 18.
'Shame', *Poetry Wales*, 5.2 (1969): 35.

'Some Place', *Mabon*, 1.1 (Spring 1969): 19.

'Symbols', *Poetry Wales*, 5.2 (1969): 36.

'The Wisdom of Eliaser', *Mabon*, 1.1 (Spring 1969): 19.

'Ynys Enlli', *Anglo-Welsh Review*, 18.41 (1969): 17.

1970

'The Bank Clerk', *Vernon Watkins 1906–1967*, ed. Leslie Norris (London: Faber, 1970): 34.

'Farm-hand', *Planet*, 1 (August/September 1970): 19.

'Nobodies', *Ishmael*, 1.1 (Autumn 1970): 9.

'Somebody', *Ishmael*, 1.1 (Autumn 1970): 10.

'Vocation', *Poetry Wales*, 6.1 (1970): 37–8.

* 'Welsh Resort', *Planet*, 1 (August/September 1970): 18.

1971

'Chat', *Poetry Wales*, 7.1 (1971): 55–6.

* 'Retrospect', *Anglo-Welsh Review*, 19.44 (1971): 73.

1972

* 'Colleague', *Poet*, 1 (Autumn 1972): 16.

'Dimensions', *Poetry Wales*, 7.4 (1972): 9.

* 'Margaret', *Second Aeon*, 15 (1972): 114.

* 'No', *Poetry Wales*, 7.4 (1972): 10.

'Now', *Poet*, 1 (Autumn 1972): 17.

* 'The Witness', *Decal Review*, 1/2 (1972): 91.

1973

'Autobiography', *Wave*, 7 (1973): 36–7.

'Inferno', *Meridian*, 1.1 (1973): 14.

'Sonata in X', *Poems '73*, ed. Gwyn Ramage (Llandysul: Gomer, 1973): 91–3. [N.B. This is a different poem from the 'Sonata in X' which appears in *Mass for Hard Times* (1992) and *Collected Later Poems 1988–2000* (2004).]

1974

'Hamlet', *Encounter*, 43.2 (1974): 92.

* 'Peep-Show', *Meridian*, 1.4 (1974): 3.

* 'Sonnet CXVI: Let me not to the marriage of true minds admit impediments…', *Poems for Shakespeare 3*, ed. Anthony Thwaite (London: The Globe Playhouse Trust, 1974): 57.

1976

* 'Pardon', *Critical Quarterly*, 18.1 (1976): 10.

'Richard Hughes', *Planet*, 33 (August 1976): 15.

* 'Star of Stage and Screen', *Poetry Wales*, 12.1 (1976): 73–4.

* 'The Steamroller Dream', *The Dragon's Hoard*, ed. Sam Adams and Gwilym Rees Hughes (Llandysul: Gomer, 1976): 36.

'Where?', *Meridian*, 8 (1976): 15.

1977

'The Climber', *In Memory of Thomas Blackburn* (London: [John Cumming], 1977): n.p.

'Dedication', *Thoth: A Morden Tower Anthology*, eds Neil Astley and Bob Lawson (Newcastle upon Tyne: Morden Tower Publications, 1977): 9.

* 'The Lecture', *Encounter*, 48.2 (1977): 41.

'Pension', *Encounter*, 49.2 (1977): 93.

'The Source', *Overland*, 68 (1977): 28.

'Staying', *Overland*, 68 (1977): 28.

1978

* 'Art', *Encounter*, 50.3 (1978): 19.

'Coming of Age', *Helix*, 2 (1978): 22.

* 'Conjunctions', *Tract*, 25 (1978): 22.

'Progressions', *Poetry in English Now*, ed. John Freeman (Cardiff: Blackweir Press, 1978): 66.

* 'Saner Than You Think', *Night Ride and Sunrise*, ed. Edward Lowbury (Aberystwyth: Celtion Press; published in association with the British Migraine Association, 1978): 45.

1979

'Appointments', *Poetry Wales*, 14.4 (1979): 7.

'Cancellation', *Poetry Wales*, 14.4 (1979): 5.

'Codex', *Poetry Wales*, 14.4 (1979): 5–6.

'Coming True', *Lettera*, 18 (1979): 89.

'Converse', *Encounter*, 52.2 (1979): 21.

'General X', *Critical Quarterly*, 21.2 (1979): 14–15.

* 'The Man in the Street', *Lettera*, 18 (1979): 88.

'Quest', *Poetry Wales*, 14.4 (1979): 10.

'Sister Non', *Poetry Wales*, 14.4 (1979): 8.

'Stop Press', *Cencrastus*, 1 (Autumn 1979): 12.

1980

* 'Boom', *Little Review*, 13–14 (1980) [Special R.S. Thomas Issue]: 3.

1981

'Excursion', *Caliban XVIII* [L'Université de Toulouse] (1981): [3].

'Grass Platforms', *A Garland for the Laureate: Poems Presented to Sir John Betjeman on his 75th Birthday* (Stratford-upon-Avon: Celandine Press, 1981).

'The New Noah', *Other Branch Readings*, 14 (Leamington Spa: Bath Place Community Arts Press, 1981): n.p.

'Predicaments', *New Leaf*, 5 (Autumn 1981): 5.

'The Tree', *Poetry Wales*, 16.3 (1981): 46.

1983

* '4004 BC', *Babel*, 1 (1983): 52.

'The Big Preachers', *Poetry Wales*, 18.3 (1983): 31.

'Cybi and Seiriol', *Poetry Wales*, 18.3 (1983): 32.

'Feminine Gender', *Poetry Wales*, 18.3 (1983): 30.

'Poets' Meeting' (Shipston-on-Stour: Celandine Press, 1983).

'Repertory', *Poetry Wales*, 18.3 (1983): 29.

'The Undying', *Anglo-Welsh Review*, 74 (1983): 35.

1984

* 'Bamboo Music', *The Cambridge 2 Poetry Magazine*, Spring 1984: 38.

* 'Candidates', *Spectrum*, 5 (1984): 32.

* 'Mae Ganddo Bleidlais', *Barn*, 256 (1984): 151. [Translation into Welsh by RST of his own poem, 'He Has the Vote', *What is a Welshman?* (Llandybie: Christopher Davies, 1974): 4.]

1986

'The Cry', *Poets Against Apartheid: An Anthology by Poets from Wales* (Cardiff: Wales Anti-Apartheid Movement, 1986): 36.

1988

* 'Brethren', *The Poetry Book Society Anthology 1988–1989*, ed. David Constantine (London: Hutchinson, 1988): 102.

'Caught', *Mir Poets*, 15 (Child Okeford, Dorset: Words Press, 1988): n.p.

* 'Looking', *The Poetry Book Society Anthology 1988–1989*, ed. David Constantine (London: Hutchinson, 1988): 101.

'The View from Europe', *Images for Africa*, ed. Jane Glencross (London: WaterAid, 1988): 15.

'A Wish', *New England Review and Breadloaf Quarterly*, 10.4 (1988): 474.

1989

'A1', *Cherwell* [Literary Supplement], 24 November 1989: [5].

'Epilogue', *Affirming Flame* (London: Community Projects Foundation, 1989): 122.

1990

'Gwallter Mechain', *Poetry Wales*, 26.1 (1990): 3–4.

'Insularities', *New Welsh Review*, 9 (Summer 1990): 16.

1991

'Cymru (Wales)', *Save the Earth*, ed. Jonathan Porritt (London: Dorling Kindersley, 1991): 92.

1992

'Wings', *Poetry Wales*, 28.2 (1992): 4. [N.B. This poem appears as 'Armistice', in *Dove-Marks on Stone: Poems for George Mackay Brown*, ed. K.A. Perryman (Schondorf: Babel, 1996): 15.]

1993

'Process', *Agenda*, 31.3 (Autumn 1993): 15.

'Sick Child', *Poetry Wales*, 29.1 (1993): 8.

* Translation from the Welsh: 'Although My Flesh Is Straw' (Ehedydd Iâl), *Planet*, 98 (April/May 1993): 42.

1995

'Born Lost', *Voices at the Door: An Anthology of Favourite Poems*, eds Owen Burt and Christine Jones (Cardiff: University of Wales Press, on behalf of Shelter Cymru, 1995): 250.

'The Lesson', *Poetry Wales*, 30.3 (1995): 24.

'Plas yn Rhiw', *The Third Day: Landscape & the Word*, ed. Kathy Miles (Llandysul: Gomer, 1995): 35. [N.B. This is a different poem from 'Plas-yn-Rhiw' in *Mass for Hard Times* (1992) and *Collected Later Poems 1988–2000* (2004).]

'A Species', *Poetry Wales*, 30.3 (1995): 23. [N.B. This is a different poem from the one with the same title in *No Truce with the Furies* (1995) and *Collected Later Poems 1988–2000* (2004).]

* Translations from the Welsh: a group of six poems chosen and translated by RST and published in *Modern Poetry in Translation*, New Series, 7 (Spring 1995: Welsh Issue, Guest Editor Dafydd Johnston): 155–61. The poems are: 'In Two Fields' (Waldo Williams); 'The Visit' (Alun Llywelyn-Williams); 'Gwladus Ddu' (G.J. Williams); 'The Shame of Llanfaes' (Gerallt Lloyd Owen); 'The Fox' and 'The Flautist' (R. Williams Parry).

* Translations of two poems by Menna Elfyn: 'Song of a Voiceless Person to British Telcom' and 'Message', *Eucalyptus: Detholiad o Gerddi / Selected Poems 1978–1994* (Llandysul: Gomer, 1995): 7, 9 and 57.

1996

'Abaty Cwm Hir', *Planet*, 116 (April/May 1996): 29.

'Calling', *Planet*, 116 (April/May 1996): 26.

'Elders', *Planet*, 116 (April/May 1996): 28.

'Filming', *Tracks*, 11 (1996): 33.

'The Gallery', *Planet*, 116 (April/May 1996): 27.

'In Memory of James and Frances Williams', *Poetry Wales*, 31.4 (1996): 53–4.

'Oil', *Agenda*, 34.1 (Spring 1996): 124.

'Story', *Drei Gedichte* (Unterreit: Antinous Presse, 1996): n.p.

'Tourney', *College Green* [Dublin: Graduate Students' Union], Summer 1996: n.p.

* 'Wood Nymph', *Drei Gedichte* (Unterreit: Antinous Presse, 1996): n.p.

1997

'The Humming Bird Never Came', *Six Poems* (Shipston-on-Stour: Celandine Press, 1997): n.p.

'Pharpar', *Six Poems* (Shipston-on-Stour: Celandine Press, 1997): n.p.

1998

'Blackbird', *Agenda*, 36.2 (Autumn 1998): 7.

'Diary', *Agenda*, 36.2 (Autumn 1998): 6.

'Dreams', *Agenda*, 36.2 (Autumn 1998): 8.

'Everywhere', *The Reader*, 2 (Spring 1998): 5.

'Island Boatman', in R.S. Thomas and Peter Hope Jones, *Between Sea and Sky: Images of Bardsey* (Llandysul: Gomer, 1998): 66.

* 'The Marksman', *Agenda*, 36.2 (Autumn 1998): 10.

'Talk', *Agenda*, 36.2 (Autumn 1998): 9.

2000

['Waiting for the tale to begin'], in R.S. Thomas, 'Time's Disc Jockey: Meditations on Some Lines in *The Anathemata*', *David Jones: Diversity in Unity*, eds Belinda Humfrey and Anne Price-Owen (Cardiff: University of Wales Press, 2000): 153.

2002

'Birthday', *Ringless Fingers* (Bangkapi: Frangipani Press, 2002): n.p. [Notes to *Ringless Fingers* suggest that this poem was composed in 1970.]

'The Father Dies', *Ringless Fingers* (Bangkapi: Frangipani Press, 2002): n.p. [Notes to *Ringless Fingers* suggest that this poem was composed in 1978.]

'Luminary', *Ringless Fingers* (Bangkapi: Frangipani Press, 2002): n.p. [Notes to *Ringless Fingers* suggest that this poem was composed in 1980.]

2003

'The Hill', *Die Vogelscheuche Nächstenliebe/Charity's Scarecrow*, ed. and trans. Kevin Perryman (Denklingen: Babel, 2003): 66.

* ['Pwy yw'r tri yn y gell...?'], in Jason Walford Davies, *Gororau'r Iaith: R.S. Thomas a'r Traddodiad Llenyddol Cymraeg* (Cardiff: University of Wales Press, 2003): 315–16.

2007

'In Memory of Ted Hughes', *Gweledigaethau: Cyfrol Deyrnged Yr Athro Gwyn Thomas*, ed. Jason Walford Davies ([Swansea]: Cyhoeddiadau Barddas, 2007): 15.

2008

['The computer is unable'], *Steinzwitschern/Stone Twittering*, ed. and trans. Kevin Perryman (Denklingen: Babel, 2008): 18.

2009

['Easter. I approach'], *The Cross*, ed. K.A. Perryman (Denklingen: Babel, 2009): n.p.

['One drop of blood'], *A Christmas Quire* (Chiang Mai and Sarn y Plas: Frangipani Press, 2009): n.p.

2010

['A bird's prayer'], *Worth 2 in the Bush* (Sarn and Chiang Mai: Frangipani Press, 2010): n.p.

['Language has run its course'], *Das Kreuz*, ed. K.A. Perryman (Denklingen, Germany: Babel, 2010): n.p.

Undated /unidentified

* 'Home Revisited' ('In the window,/In the absence of aspidistra...'), 1960s.

'The Orphan', post 1971.

'Pact', poem in CND Cymru birthday card, ?1980s.